The

2008
Checking In

52 FAVORITE PLACES TO STAY IN NEW ENGLAND

Published by *The Boston Globe*

The Boston Globe

Copyright © 2007 by the Boston Globe. All rights reserved. No part of this publication may be reproduced, stored in a retrieval system, or transmitted in any form by any means, electronic, mechanical, photocopying, or otherwise, without prior written permission of the publisher, The Boston Globe, PO Box 55819 Boston, MA 02205-5819.
This book is available in quantity at special discounts for your group or organization. For further information, contact:

The Boston Globe Store
PO Box 55819
Boston, MA 02205-5819
Phone: (888) 665-2667
Fax: (617) 929-7636
www.BostonGlobeStore.com

Printed in U.S.A.
ISBN 13: 978-0-9790137-4-4

The factual information listed in this guidebook was confirmed at press time, but is subject to change. We therefore recommend that you call ahead or visit each lodging establishment online for the most up-to-date rates and other information. Reviews reflect the experiences and opinions of the writers, which may or may not match reader experiences and opinions.

EDITOR Janice Page
DESIGNER Rena Anderson Sokolow
ASSISTANT EDITOR Ron Driscoll

SPECIAL THANKS The Boston Globe Travel Department; Nancy Callahan, MacDonald & Evans

COVER PHOTO Provincetown provides the perfect Cape Cod getaway. In summer 2007, Roger Pageau, Grand Treasurer of the Grand Lodge of Masons in Massachusetts, smiles in the shadow of the Pilgrim Monument while participating in ceremonial festivities. Photo by Vincent DeWitt for the Boston Globe.

Welcome

to the second edition of "Checking In: 52 Favorite Places to Stay in New England," your guide to some of the most memorable getaways in and around Boston. We don't really expect you to get away every weekend of the year, but we do hope you'll find your perfect home away from home in these pages, no matter what season you choose for your escape. ❖ In 2004, The Boston Globe introduced a feature in the Sunday Travel section called "Checking In" where, much as a music or theater critic evaluates a performance, an inn or B&B reviewer takes the measure of the total lodging experience. As in the first edition of our guide, reviewers have chosen destinations with the twin goals of finding distinctive, affordable lodging while offering a mix of locations throughout New England. Reviewers do not reveal their intent when booking, they pay for rooms and meals (when a restaurant is on-site, they try to eat there), and they in turn are reimbursed by the Globe. ❖ Whether your destination is an island off the coast of Maine, the urban bustle of Boston, or the foothills of the Green Mountains, you're likely to discover a place that suits you. Open to any page, and you'll become immersed in the stories and the atmosphere of the places we've visited. You'll find "the scent of lilacs mingling with the salt-tinged air of Casco Bay," or an inn with "a restaurant along the water's edge that serves both grilled salmon and peanut-butter-and-jelly sandwiches." Read how one couple put off retirement to restore and run two historic homes in Providence, and why a globe-trotting proprietor's B&B "feels more like an expatriate hangout than a genteel inn." ❖ The wide array of lodging reflects our reviewers' varied tastes. Whether they lean toward contemporary or Victorian décor, are on the lookout for a family-friendly place, or have an appreciation for a particular inn's history, they are all attracted to a warm, welcoming attitude. We're confident that holds for you, too. Happy travels.

The Boston Globe Travel Department

The Chanler at Cliff Walk

Getaway 1

117 Memorial Boulevard,
Newport, R.I.
866-793-5664 or 401-847-1300
www.thechanler.com

RATES
20 rooms. Doubles $275-$1,195.

WHAT WE LIKED MOST
The luxury bath with double Jacuzzi, glass-enclosed shower with body jets, and heated tile floors.

WHAT WE LIKED LEAST
Realizing we couldn't afford to stay more than one night.

WHAT SURPRISED US
A level of staffing so generous there was someone stationed at the door to greet us each time we went out and returned.

YOU KNOW YOU'RE AT THE CHANLER WHEN... *you need to keep reminding yourself you aren't staying at the Newport mansion of a fabulously wealthy friend.*

THINGS TO REMEMBER

MAINE · NEW HAMPSHIRE · VERMONT · MASS

AT THE CHANLER, I did something I have never done before: I watched a flat-screen television from a Jacuzzi tub. This may not seem like a big deal, but I rarely watch television. Here, though, it seemed the height of luxury. ❖ The bath was the most indulgent aspect of our room in what was the first mansion on Newport's famous Cliff Walk. Overlooking Easton's Beach, the mansion was built around 1862 for John Winthrop Chanler, a congressman from New York, and his wife, Margaret Astor Ward. Its current design dates from a renovation around the turn of the last century. It still feels more mansion than hotel, with high ceilings, fabric wall coverings, and sparkling chandeliers. ❖ In addition to the oversized whirlpool and wall-mounted TV, our bath had heated tile floors and a spacious glass-enclosed shower with a regular spigot, three body jets, and a rainfall showerhead. A deep sink set into a hand-painted vanity with a bow front provided plenty of storage space. ❖ Our room, The Federal, was large and beautifully furnished (all Chanler rooms and suites are decorated to reflect a certain theme or historical period). The centerpiece was a queen-size bed with a canopy of shirred fabric caught by a big center knot underneath and valances in a burgundy, blue, and green pattern along the perimeter. ❖ A door with wooden shutters led to a rooftop patio overlooking the ocean; the patio was glassed in below the railing to cut the wind and furnished with a table and chairs. ❖ Thoughtful touches were everywhere: A chunky pewter clock (not the ubiquitous digital clock radio) sat on the nightstand. A button on the wall activated a "do not disturb" or "service, please" light outside the door. ❖ We arrived to a welcome treat of fresh blueberries, strawberries, and blackberries topped with shaved coconut. After dinner, we came back to robes laid out on the bed, slippers set on a linen napkin on the floor, two chocolates, and a card with the following day's weather report. ❖ Breakfast was in the Verandah, with an expansive view of the ocean, beach, and grounds. Tables were set with white linens, crystal, and silver. An assortment of breads, pastries, fruit, and yogurt is complimentary for inn guests, and there is an a la carte menu as well. ❖ As luxurious as our room was, it is one of The Chanler's more modest accommodations. At the top of the line are "villa" rooms featuring private entrances, hot tubs, enclosed courtyards, and ocean or garden views.

ELLEN ALBANESE, *Globe Staff*

The Inn at Sawmill Farm

Getaway 2

Crosstown Road,
West Dover, Vt.
800-493-1133 or 802-464-8131
www.theinnatsawmillfarm.com

RATES
20 rooms. $300-$850; includes breakfast, afternoon tea in fall and winter, and five-course dinner for two.

WHAT WE LIKED MOST
Interesting assortment of current magazines in our room.

WHAT WE LIKED LEAST
Having to leave mental bread crumbs to retrace our steps through the labyrinth of halls and stairs.

WHAT SURPRISED US
Great wine list that ranges from trophy grand cru Bordeaux to food-friendly Sardinian vermentino.

YOU KNOW YOU'RE AT THE INN AT SAWMILL FARM WHEN ... *the grandfather clock chimes (accurately) in the cathedral-ceiling lounge.*

THINGS TO REMEMBER
_____
_____
_____

MAINE · NEW HAMPSHIRE · **VERMONT** · MASS

WE DIDN'T MEET INTERIOR DECORATOR Ione Williams during our stay at The Inn at Sawmill Farm, but we know the woman loves roses. ❖ She and her architect husband, Rodney, bought this rural farmhouse and barn in 1967 and transformed it into an inn, with Ione handling the decor. ❖ We're surprised she didn't call it "La Vie en Rose," but that might have lacked the proper rural-chic ring for ski country. Still, the rose-pattern wallpaper, upholstery, and draperies made us anticipate Edith Piaf every time the inn's background music changed. It's a motif that's worn well in this rambling inn. At the end of the day, the effect is a cultured country ambience enhanced by a blazing fireplace in the main lounge, plush mattresses and voluptuous bed linens in the rooms, and a full-bore, old-fashioned haute dining experience as retro as the roses. ❖ Our room, No. 12, had floral wallpaper — roses, of course — on two walls. The bed coverlet, headboard canopy, three comfortable padded chairs and voluminous Roman shades all matched the wallpaper. A spritz of rose scent and we could have imagined ourselves in a garden. The masterfully constructed shades kept out the cold from a wall of windows and set of doors leading out onto a private deck. ❖ Only one room in the main inn has a television, but addicts can repair to the library — in the former hayloft — where couches and chairs are arrayed around the TV. The hayloft looks down onto the lounge area in the former barn, where non-mealtime activity centers on the big brick fireplace accented with copper pots, pans, and kettles.
❖ The dining room was also once part of the barn, as the timbered cathedral ceiling and one wall of rough boards attests. (The other walls are covered in … rose floral wallpaper.) ❖ We suspect that many guests at the inn come less for the nearby Mount Snow ski trails than for now-chef/proprietor Brill Williams's food and the convenience of not having to drive home after sampling the spectacular wine list. While Williams cooks in classic haute cuisine style, his commitment to using local ingredients whenever possible gives a feeling of rustic feast to the meals.
❖ A note on dessert: The signature chocolate sauce served on ice cream (one dessert option) is so good that the inn sells it by the jar. ❖ We thought we'd never eat again — until we saw the breakfast menu. Scrambled eggs with white truffle butter and onion brioche set a new standard for the morning repast. Truly la vie en rose.

PATRICIA HARRIS AND DAVID LYON, *Globe Correspondents*

Three Stallion Inn

Getaway 3

665 Stock Farm Road,
Randolph, Vt.
800-424-5575 or 802-728-5575
www.3stallioninn.com

RATES
14 rooms. $150-$225.

WHAT WE LIKED MOST
The hiking trails, so close and yet so far from any sign of civilization that we got deeply lost ... for a while.

WHAT WE LIKED LEAST
The rooms are rather plain, with bathrooms tending toward the quality of an inexpensive motel.

WHAT SURPRISED US
How much open land there was available for all the outdoor activities.

YOU KNOW YOU'RE AT THREE STALLION INN WHEN ... suddenly, around 6 p.m., seemingly from nowhere on this lonely stretch of road, crowds gather to feast at Lippitt's Restaurant.

THINGS TO REMEMBER

MAINE • NEW HAMPSHIRE • **VERMONT** • MASS

WHETHER THE STATE IS READY to admit it or not, global warming is already having an impact on tourists who come here to ski. ❖ So while we had come to Randolph in March to ski (the town is an easy drive from Killington, Mad River Glen, Stowe, and Sugarbush), we had the foresight to throw our hiking boots in the car, because we had heard that the 40 miles of cross-country and snowshoe trails surrounding the Three Stallion Inn could also be hiked. ❖ Turned out there was not a speck of snow to be seen, but the hiking was terrific. The trailhead was across the road from the Morgan House, an old farmhouse that is part of the inn, and where we stayed. The inn's main building, itself an old farmhouse, was built along with the Morgan House in the late 1800s, and both interiors retain the heavy, dark-wood feel of the Victorian period. Some of the bathrooms are being updated with porcelain tile and granite vanity sinks. ❖ Our room (No. 10, the "Honeymoon Room") was large, with a king-size bed, a little alcove with a loveseat, and its own porches both front and back. The exteriors of both the main inn and the Morgan House are prettier than the interiors, which are basic country farmhouse style. ❖ The inn is part of the Green Mountain Stock Farm, 1,300 acres of countryside that owners Sam and Jinny Sammis are selling as 10- to 100-acre lots for residential development. The few new houses that were standing when we were there looked out on woods and mountains and were not visible from the inn. ❖ Mountain biking is another popular activity. In addition to the inn's 40 miles of biking trails, the White River Valley Trails Association offers 265 miles of mapped trails just out the back door. The inn's trout pond is stocked for guests to practice catch-and-release skills; you can also book a personalized, Orvis-equipped fly-fishing trip on the nearby White River with the inn's Orvis-trained fishing guide. ❖ Given the inn's name, we thought horseback riding might be offered, but the horses on the premises are boarding animals and not available for guests to ride. Three Stallion Inn descends from the stallions that Justin Morgan raised when he lived near here in the late 1700s. The oldest of all American breeds, the Morgan horse has retained its identity for more than 200 years.❖ The inn's Lippitt's Restaurant draws people from towns all around Randolph with its exceptional cuisine, termed "American regional."

JULIE HATFIELD, *Globe Correspondent*

Norumbega Inn

Getaway 4

*63 High St.,
Camden, Maine
877-363-4646 or 207-236-4646
www.norumbegainn.com*

RATES
12 rooms. $155-$475.

WHAT WE LIKED MOST
The ample public space, with nooks and alcoves aplenty for reading spots.

WHAT WE LIKED LEAST
The fireplaces were not working the weekend of our visit.

WHAT SURPRISED US
How quickly time passes in a castle on a winter weekend.

YOU KNOW YOU'RE AT THE NORUMBEGA INN WHEN ... *a man's home is your castle.*

THINGS TO REMEMBER

MAINE · **NEW HAMPSHIRE** · **VERMONT** · **MASS**

WITH ITS STONE FACADE, midnight-blue trim, and towering turret, the Norumbega Inn has the imposing appearance of a medieval castle, where a king might have plotted the start of an empire. ❖ No doubt, the Norumbega's designer and first owner, Joseph Barker Stearns, intended to make a splash in 1886 with his home perched high above Penobscot Bay. The farm-boy-turned-wealthy-inventor had toured Europe and taken close notice of its castles. White clapboard and symmetry still dominated the architectural landscape of Maine, and Stearns departed tradition with hulking stone and jaunty angles. ❖ As if to underscore his point, Stearns chose a worthy name for his mansion, Norumbega, after the mythical New World city where homes were said to have pillars of gold and natives carried quarts of pearls on their heads. It is a place that is at once grand and creaky, studiously proper and idiosyncratic, starting with its abundance of nooks and alcoves. The Norumbega has just 12 guest rooms, but it is sprawling. There is a generous amount of common space, including five downstairs rooms, and the shared areas create a convivial spirit among guests. Shortly after our arrival, a couple invited us to join their improvised game of backgammon in the library, a rounded room that fills out the turret. ❖ The setting was unexpectedly cozy. As the wind howled against the stone walls, sconces threw warm light, heat pumped generously, and a dining room sideboard remained stocked with hot beverages and inn-made cookies. We might have stayed put all night, but the Norumbega does not serve dinner. So we bundled against the dipping temperatures and made the roughly half-mile trek into town along a boulevard of pristinely kept houses. We had reservations at the Francine Bistro, and the trip was worth it, especially for the grilled lamb with golden raisin polenta. ❖ Breakfast is served from 8 to 9:30 and offered good reason to rise. Courses arrive in unhurried succession in the solarium, which has water views, a slanted ceiling, and six tables. The evening's rain had turned to snow, and after breakfast we strolled the inn's three acres, which had been transformed by a coating of white. When we returned, the other guests had departed. We knew we ought to be going, too, but we helped ourselves to one more cup of tea. ❖ I thought about Stearns's trajectory from farm boy to estate owner. I imagined him sitting in his music room surveying all that was his to enjoy. And now, his castle was ours, shared only with the wind and the snow whirling just outside.

SARAH SCHWEITZER, *Globe Staff*

Tolland Inn

Getaway 5

63 Tolland Green,
Tolland, Conn.
860-872-0800 or 877-465-0800
www.tollandinn.com

RATES
Doubles $95-$229 with full breakfast.

WHAT WE LIKED MOST
The warmth and friendliness of the innkeepers.

WHAT WE LIKED LEAST
The size of our room; next time we will choose one of the spacious suites on the second floor.

WHAT SURPRISED US
How large and comfortable the sunken hot tub was, with steps and a handrail.

YOU KNOW YOU'RE AT THE TOLLAND INN WHEN... no matter which room you book, you sleep in a bed custom-made by innkeeper and furniture maker Steve Beeching.

THINGS TO REMEMBER

WHEN WE ARRIVED AT THE TOLLAND on a Friday evening, innkeeper Steve Beeching welcomed us warmly. He showed us where breakfast would be served, gave us a key to our room, recommended a place for dinner, then quietly disappeared.
❖ We had no idea of the extent to which Beeching's talents and interests would color nearly every aspect of our weekend stay.
❖ We slept (as all the guests do) in a bed made in Beeching's workshop. We ate at a table he designed and built. We breakfasted on Belgian waffles and orange-stuffed French toast he prepared, all the while admiring his Impressionistic oil paintings on the dining room walls. ❖ Steve and his wife, Susan, bought the inn in 1985, renovated it, and opened it two years later. Though Susan comes from a line of innkeepers (her mother and grandmother owned inns on Nantucket), she is the first to admit that Steve runs the show at the Tolland Inn. Susan has a remarkable talent for engaging guests in conversation, often sharing tales of her "real life" as a second-grade teacher, and her voluble charm complements her husband's reserve. On busy Sunday mornings, her pupils sometimes help serve breakfast. ❖ Listed on the National Register of Historic Places, the inn is located across from the scenic Tolland Green, which boasts several historic buildings dating from Colonial times. Guests are welcome to use a sunporch decorated with grapevine wreaths and pierced-tin lamps and warmed by a fireplace Steve built using bricks from a chimney removed during the renovation. There also is a parlor with a Victorian daybed (again Steve's handiwork) and a tea table stocked with an impressive variety of teas and homemade chocolate chip cookies. ❖ Our room, one of two on the first floor, had its own entrance from the porch. Though it abutted the dining room, a double door insulated sound. ❖ The room was small but comfortable. In addition to Steve's four-poster queen-size canopy bed, it featured a highboy and space-conserving shelf tables, all with a distinctive scallop shell design. The highlight of the bath was a large, kidney-shaped hot tub in a cozy alcove with pierced-tin lights and wall maps of Guadeloupe and St. Martin. In many historic properties we've visited, there is one heating system for the whole building. Here, not only was there a thermostat in our room, there was a separate thermostat in the bath. ❖ Steve's woodworking skills extend well beyond the inn. His furniture is in homes across the country and in Japan and Italy.

ELLEN ALBANESE, *Globe Staff*

Old Inn on the Green

Getaway 6

134 Hartsville-New Marlborough Road, New Marlborough, Mass.
413-229-7924
www.oldinn.com

RATES
11 rooms. $205-$380.

WHAT WE LIKED MOST
An unforced sense of history.

WHAT WE LIKED LEAST
Voices carried from bar and kitchen to our bedroom.

WHAT SURPRISED US
High quality of dining room food and service for the bargain price.

YOU KNOW YOU'RE AT THE OLD INN ON THE GREEN WHEN... *you feel you might need trekking poles to climb the stairs.*

THINGS TO REMEMBER
_____
_____
_____
_____
_____

MAINE · NEW HAMPSHIRE · VERMONT · MASS

CANDLELIGHT IS FLATTERING — maybe that's why people of a certain age choose to celebrate birthdays and anniversaries at the Old Inn on the Green. This 1760 stagecoach stop turned inn and restaurant doesn't overdo the electricity. ❖ True to its name, the white clapboard building with a long, columned front porch sits at the head of the green in this tranquil southern Berkshires village. The wide, worn, and warped floorboards attest to its age. So does the steep staircase that leads from the front entry hall to the bedrooms on the second floor. "It's typical of old buildings," chef and co-owner Peter Platt told us. "It's more like climbing a hill than a flight of stairs." ❖ According to Platt, the structure has been a tavern, a store, a post office, and a boarding house. When previous owners opened the restaurant in 1982, they accentuated the building's venerable past by lighting the four dining rooms with candles and firelight only. All four, each with a fireplace, remain electricity-free. ❖ Our room, No. 191, was situated on a back corner where the winter afternoon light streamed in the 12-over-12 windows along one wall. In fact, the modern world barely intruded. The white walls were trimmed with moldings in a teal green that would be right at home at Sturbridge Village. A cozy alcove held a single bed, while an armchair and sofa bed formed a little sitting area. Extra blankets and battery-powered lanterns were tucked in a handsome, country-style armoire. ❖ Our room did have electricity, but the two wall-mounted reading lamps and two small table lamps were not especially intrusive. Only two items of modern technology marred the timeless set piece: a hair dryer mounted on the bathroom wall above a distressed wooden washstand (the room also had a pedestal sink and big shower with wooden walls), and two cordless phones in the bedroom.
❖ It took a bit of twisting and turning to read the dinner menu in the candlelight of the dining room, but it wasn't hard to tell that Platt's midweek three-course dinner special was a good deal on artful fare from one of the Berkshires' most celebrated chefs. (Platt headed the kitchen at the famed Wheatleigh Hotel in Lenox for 12 years.) ❖ New white tapers were already lighted when we returned to the dining room for breakfast. Co-owner Meredith Kennard poured juice, brewed pots of French press coffee, and presented a basket of hot croissants, muffins, and scones included with the lodging. (Other cooked breakfast entrees are available a la carte.)

PATRICIA HARRIS AND DAVID LYON, *Globe Correspondents*

Homestead Inn

Getaway 7

420 Field Point Road,
Greenwich, Conn.
203-869-7500
www.homesteadinn.com

RATES
18 rooms. $250-$495, breakfast not included.

WHAT WE LIKED MOST
The heated terra cotta floor tiles in the bedroom and bathroom could be controlled by a thermostat.

WHAT WE LIKED LEAST
Breakfast is not included in the price of the room.

WHAT SURPRISED US
How close the inn is to Interstate 95 and yet it feels like a country estate.

YOU KNOW YOU'RE AT HOMESTEAD INN WHEN ... *you can dine on sumptuous French cuisine at the restaurant named for the owner, Thomas Henkelmann.*

THINGS TO REMEMBER
_____
_____
_____
_____

MAINE • NEW HAMPSHIRE • VERMONT • MASS

NOT FAR FROM INTERSTATE 95, a two-lane road winds past stately homes in the Belle Haven neighborhood. At the crest of a hill, on a 3-acre property, the Homestead Inn stands like a festive cake. The original 18th-century farmhouse was enhanced in 1859 in an Italianate Gothic style, complete with a squat, square cupola and decorative brackets under the eaves. ❖ The latest incarnation of this lovely structure came in 1997, when Thomas Henkelmann and his wife Theresa opened the Homestead Inn and its restaurant, which shares its name with the owner. The inn and restaurant are a perfect marriage of comfort and fine cuisine, as exemplified by Thomas — a classically trained chef who has worked in France, Switzerland, and his native Germany — and Theresa, an interior designer who had her own firm in New York for many years. ❖ Theresa designed all 18 rooms in the inn. Her knowledge of furniture and fabrics and her eye for detail helped to create imaginative spaces that combine traditional decorating sensibilities with whimsy and a sense of humor. ❖ Guest Chamber 115 has warm, mustard yellow walls, white double-louvered doors, a queen-size bed with an elaborate carved French oak headboard, and a matching carved armoire that hides the TV. ❖ Bright landscapes and a still life — real paintings, not reproductions — enliven the walls, along with a wide-rimmed mirror with subtle images of Chinese peasant scenes. The bed's quilted coverlet is white with scalloped edges; the sham and pillows are a loose geometric weave in ivory, moss, and salmon. White-checked Fili D'oro linens are 100 percent cotton and 1,000 percent luxurious. ❖ An oriental carpet rests on large terra cotta tiles that extend into the spacious bathroom. On a cold winter afternoon, I was delighted to discover the tiles could be heated via a thermostat. ❖ The overall effect is one of lush Colonialism with a contemporary edge, though this is not the case in other guest chambers, each of which has its own distinct style. Thomas Henkelmann, the restaurant, accounts for 80 percent of the inn's business, according to Theresa. After tasting the food, I can see why. ❖ "The food here is like being in France. There are no hints of fusion. It's contemporary French cuisine, light and pure in its essence," she said. ❖ Breakfast is not included, but it is worth the addition to your bill. My poached egg with a potato pancake was perfection, and the coffee was strong and good. There wasn't anything else I needed, except perhaps a few more days to indulge in luxury.

NECEE REGIS, *Globe Correspondent*

The Inn
at Thorn Hill and Spa

Getaway 8

40 Thorn Hill Road,
Jackson Village, N.H.
800-289-8990 or 603-383-4242
www.innatthornhill.com

RATES
22 rooms, six open seasonally.
$169-$430, including meals.

WHAT WE LIKED MOST
The room rate included breakfast, afternoon tea, and a three-course dinner.

WHAT WE LIKED LEAST
The tiny waiting area for the spa.

WHAT SURPRISED US
How far in advance it was necessary to reserve dining and spa times.

YOU KNOW YOU'RE AT THE INN AT THORN HILL AND SPA WHEN... *even the smallest room in the main inn has a gas fireplace and Jacuzzi for two.*

THINGS TO REMEMBER
_____
_____
_____
_____

MAINE • **NEW HAMPSHIRE** • VERMONT • MASS

LITTLE THINGS MAKE A BIG DIFFERENCE, and at the Inn at Thorn Hill and Spa, no detail is overlooked. From the moment we arrived until we departed, we felt welcomed and pampered by a trained, service-oriented staff that was friendly but professional, helpful but not overbearing. ❖ Sure, the high-thread-count sheets and down comforters were nice, as were the in-room gas fireplace and whirlpool tub for two, but it is the warm, attentive service that makes the Inn at Thorn Hill special. ❖ We are not the only ones who have noticed. Recently, Travel & Leisure magazine readers named it one of the Top 100 hotels not just in the United States and Canada, but in the world. With such recognition, one might expect room rates in the stratosphere. But it is possible to stay for less than $200 a night with breakfast, afternoon tea, and a three-course dinner for two included. Setting the inn apart are innkeepers Jim and Ibby Cooper, who have owned it since 1992. One Cooper or the other is always present, keeping watch over the myriad details that make or break a guest's visit. ❖ In 2002, a fire severely damaged the inn. Encouraged by an outpouring of support from friends, neighbors, and former guests, the Coopers rebuilt. Working with their architect, they created an inn that honors its original gable-roofed design, yet allows for the modern conveniences and amenities that guests of four-diamond properties demand. We booked the Mt. Pierce Room on the second floor of the main inn — one of the least-expensive and smallest rooms — but the amenities and service were still expansive. Our room had a queen-size bed topped with a plump comforter, television with a DVD player, gas fireplace, bathroom with a two-person Jacuzzi and a separate shower. Only the view was so-so. ❖ We enjoyed the inn's extensive common spaces, and I enjoyed a combo massage and facial for $99 at the spa. That facility is squeezed into the basement, with a tiny waiting area that lacks privacy. But I quibble: The services are professional, and my treatments left me dreamy and glowing. ❖ On the reservation clerk's advice, I made both dinner and spa reservations when I booked our room. The quality and presentation of chef Jonathan Cox's indulgent three-course dinners were sublime. Oenophiles should take time to tour the 3,000-bottle wine cellar and ask about wine dinners. ❖ Breakfast, too, is a culinary delight. On our last morning, out of the corner of my eye I caught Ibby Cooper, passing through the dining room, quietly noting every detail.

HILARY NANGLE, *Globe Correspondent*

Village Inn of Woodstock

Getaway 9

*41 Pleasant St.,
Woodstock, Vt.
800-722-4571
www.villageinnofwoodstock.com*

RATES
Eight rooms. $150-$320.

WHAT WE LIKED MOST
Carefully assembled, satisfying homemade breakfasts served by good-humored hosts.

WHAT WE LIKED LEAST
The more-is-more decorating philosophy, especially where it comes to Bradbury & Bradbury wallpaper.

WHAT SURPRISED US
The large number of foods made better by a dollop of Woodstock Water Buffalo yogurt.

YOU KNOW YOU'RE AT THE VILLAGE INN OF WOODSTOCK WHEN . . . *your turndown service comes with a note card that reads "Sweet Dreams from Spanky."*

THINGS TO REMEMBER
_____
_____
_____
_____
_____

MAINE • NEW HAMPSHIRE • **VERMONT** • MASS

BY THE TIME WE GOT TO WOODSTOCK, we were full of cheese.
❖ Maybe that's not as poetic as the trip Joni Mitchell wrote about in 1969, but since Yasgur's Farm and that other Woodstock are a long way from the maple-and-dairy gantlet that leads to Vermont's Village Inn of Woodstock, my husband and I were feeling pretty satisfied with the way our weekend had started out.
❖ On the journey up from Boston, we'd gone out of our way to sample parts of the Vermont Cheese Trail, and the result was some terrific backroads scenery, free snacking, and, as they say in "The Ten Commandments," very much cattle. We had chosen to stay at the pink, Victorian-era inn because it was situated on the outskirts of the quaint shopping district and because innkeeper Evelyn Brey, both helpful and good-humored on the phone, seemed up to delivering on her promise of sumptuous, three-course, homemade breakfasts. Since vacancies were limited, we shifted rooms mid-stay — not ideal, but Brey's efficiency made the transition painless. ❖ Room 2 was a cozy, surprisingly quiet chamber on the second floor at the front of the house. An explosion of wallpaper combined with heavy drapes, fake flower arrangements, and dark floorboards covered by a formal area rug might make some guests feel boxed in, and they'll get no relief from the small-but-functional, shower-only bathroom. We were happy to trade up to Room 9 for our second night. ❖ This third-floor space, despite being defined by the slope of the roofline, had airiness and warmth to match its soft metallic wallpaper. The bathroom was again too small for a tub (other accommodations do offer whirlpools and more luxury), but this one featured a larger shower with nicer fixtures, soapstone and marble tiles, a square pedestal sink, and ample shelving. The inn has a couple of comfy porches as well as a garden patio sitting area that invites al fresco eating in the summer months, which brings us to the real attraction here: breakfast. ❖ Brey, a former banker, does all the baking and serving. Her husband, David (a former car salesman), cooks made-to-order entrees such as omelets and Belgian waffles. In their formal, fireside dining room laden with still more antiques and flowered fabrics, your day might begin with a poached pear dressed in rich Woodstock Water Buffalo yogurt, followed by a perfect sour-cream coffeecake, nutty granola with strawberries, oatmeal toast slathered in blackberry jam, and quiche amped up with goat cheese and flecks of jalapeno. Even the decaf coffee is complex and satisfying.

JANICE PAGE, *Globe Staff*

Grand Pequot Tower

Getaway 10

Foxwoods Resort Casino
Route 2, Ledyard, Conn.
800-369-9663
www.foxwoods.com

RATES
824 rooms and suites. $165-$375.

WHAT WE LIKED MOST
The wide range of restaurant choices inside the resort complex.

WHAT WE LIKED LEAST
The confusing maze of finding the hotel front desk from the parking garage.

WHAT SURPRISED US
Free indoor parking.

YOU KNOW YOU'RE AT GRAND PEQUOT TOWER WHEN... *you can eat breakfast or bet on card games around the clock.*

THINGS TO REMEMBER

MAINE • NEW HAMPSHIRE • VERMONT • MASS

WE HAVE TO ADMIT THAT "the wonder of it all" has long been lost on us, but Foxwoods Resort's 15th anniversary seemed like a good excuse to take a closer look at the gaming and entertainment star shining over the woods of eastern Connecticut. Like so many ventures, timing is everything.

❖ We didn't get our money down fast enough to snag a room on Valentine's Day at the flagship Grand Pequot Tower hotel, which opened in 1997, so we settled instead for the Monday of Valentine's week. ❖ On the drive down, we managed to take a couple of wrong turns, but once we got within 20 miles, all we had to do was follow the stream of buses bringing day-trippers to the complex. To be perfectly honest, the whole complex is more tasteful than anything in Vegas. The hotel lobby is a gently glamorous, sweeping expanse of marble floors and wood-paneled walls. Light funnels down through a central skylight in the rotunda to illuminate the first of many Native American sculptures sprinkled throughout the resort as a nod to tribal affiliation. ❖ The hotel lobby (there is a separate lobby for arriving bus groups) sits two floors below the crowds and diversions of the gaming halls, shops, and most of the resort's restaurants. Our quarters, Room 1939, proved an equally peaceful oasis with a floor-to-ceiling window at the front of the hotel where we could watch the steady stream of cars and buses flowing into Foxwoods.

❖ The room was designed to soothe with a complex neutral palette: beige textured vinyl wallpaper, beige floral bedspread, and a beige-and-brown diamond pattern carpet. It was an altogether comfortable space, though, like most Foxwoods visitors, we didn't plan to spend a lot of time there.

❖ Paragon, the high-rolling gourmet restaurant on the 24th floor of the casino tower, was closed on a Monday night. We decided to share several dishes in a cozy booth in the Golden Dragon, which serves Chinese food with a Korean accent. The sliced pork in garlic sauce was dark, spicy, and authentically Chinese. The westernized cashew shrimp and chicken dish made a perfect milder counterpoint. ❖ We did manage to escape with a loss of only seven quarters at the slot machines. More dedicated players were still hunched over the blackjack tables when we called it a night. Some of them (or people who looked just like them) were still there in the morning.

PATRICIA HARRIS AND DAVID LYON, *Globe Correspondents*

Ash Street Inn

Getaway 11

118 Ash St.,
Manchester, N.H.
603-668-9908
www.ashstreetinn.com

RATES
Five rooms. $139-$189.

WHAT WE LIKED MOST
The sophistication and amenities of a high-end-hotel in an intimate bed-and-breakfast setting.

WHAT WE LIKED LEAST
That we couldn't make a reservation for Saturday afternoon tea on short notice.

WHAT SURPRISED US
That an urban inn could be so comfortable, cozy, and charming.

YOU KNOW YOU'RE AT THE ASH STREET INN WHEN... *you enter this elegant Victorian house and forget you're in the city.*

THINGS TO REMEMBER
_____
_____
_____
_____

MAINE • NEW HAMPSHIRE • VERMONT • MASS

I

LIKE MANY PEOPLE, I tend to think of B&Bs as destinations for romantic getaways, not places to stay on the road for business. The Ash Street Inn has completely changed that mindset.

❖ This classy urban inn, in a three-story Queen Anne Victorian, was a beauty in distress when Eric and Darlene Johnston bought it seven years ago. Built as a private home in 1885, it later became a rooming house, a hair salon, an art studio, and a dermatologist's office, all of which took their toll. By the time the Johnstons came on the scene, the decaying house had broken windows, asbestos siding, and a porch nearly devoured by carpenter ants. Gorgeous oak doors, stunning hardwood floors, ornamental woodwork, and breathtaking stained glass hinted at its original grandeur.

❖ The Johnstons, refugees from the corporate world, had the time, taste, and money to restore that glory. Whole sections of the interior were gutted, wiring and plumbing were updated, siding was removed to reveal original shingling, and a new kitchen and bathrooms were installed. According to the Johnstons, they bought the house for $175,000 and spent another $500,000 renovating it. When the inn finally opened, the couple aimed to recoup their costs by renting all of their rooms every night. Imagine their dismay when, in the inn's early days, between four and seven rooms were occupied — per month. Eventually, though, business began humming. ❖ Each beautifully furnished room has a private bathroom, queen-size bed, down pillows and blankets, triple sheeting, monogrammed robes, filtered and softened water, and wireless Internet. The inn also provides complimentary airport pickup and drop-off, and free local transportation.

Eric is the more extroverted half of this innkeeping couple, but he sensed when we wanted to talk and when we preferred to be left alone. He is also the cook and makes delicious buttermilk pancakes with spiced apples, French toast, scrambled eggs, and veggie omelets. He will even prepare brown-bag breakfasts to go for travelers on early flights (the inn is 10 minutes from the Manchester-Boston Regional Airport). Throughout the day, he bakes cookies, muffins (including cinnamon-pecan), and mini-scones (buttermilk, raisin, orange-chocolate, and apricot-white chocolate) for munching, and guests are welcome to raid the kitchen refrigerator for drinks and snacks. ❖ The inn is located within walking distance of downtown Manchester in a neighborhood where homes and businesses coexist. In the inn's guest book, a visitor from Georgia nicely captured the essence of this place. ❖ "What do you get when you cross a five-star hotel with your grandmother's home?" he wrote. His answer: the Ash Street Inn.

SACHA PFEIFFER, *Globe Staff*

Blueberry Cove Inn

Getaway 12

75 Kingstown Road,
Narragansett, R.I.
401-792-9865 or 800-478-1426
www.blueberrycoveinn.com

RATES
Eight doubles and one two-bedroom suite. $140-$250.

WHAT WE LIKED MOST
The oversized whirlpool tub with powerful jets and comfortable design.

WHAT WE LIKED LEAST
The plain appearance of our room and the need for some minor repairs.

WHAT SURPRISED US
The availability of a guest computer in the parlor and wireless access throughout the inn.

YOU KNOW YOU'RE AT BLUEBERRY COVE INN WHEN... it's a short walk to funky shops, several restaurants, and one of Rhode Island's best beaches.

THINGS TO REMEMBER

MAINE · NEW HAMPSHIRE · VERMONT · MASS

WE CAME FOR THE CHOCOLATE, but we would come back for the beach. ❖ We have had our eye on the Blueberry Cove Inn for some time; the promise of comfortable rooms with private baths in a Victorian home just four blocks from the ocean seemed appealing. But the promise of nonstop chocolate treats on the weekend following Valentine's Day pulled us over the edge. ❖ The inn always offers a chocolate weekend in February and adds similarly themed events when the mood strikes, said David Gerraughty, who owns the property with his wife, Seely. The Gerraughtys will also host a "chocolate slumber party" at any time for a group renting four or more rooms. ❖ Upon our arrival Friday evening, we were presented with a smorgasbord of chocolate delights. We quickly dove into a mint chocolate mousse with whipped topping, tunneled through a fudge cake until we reached the raspberry cream center, and admired heart-shaped chocolate chip cheesecakes made red with a topping of raspberry syrup (OK, after we admired them, we ate them). Saturday afternoon brought cannolis with chocolate chip filling, mini eclairs, white and dark chocolate brownies, and chocolate chip cookies. A similar smorgasbord was set out Saturday evening. Seely makes all the chocolate treats. ❖ Much as we love chocolate, what most impressed us was the inn's location, a few blocks from Narragansett Town Beach and within easy walking distance of shops and restaurants. ❖ Our room, the Lighthouse Whirlpool Room, was smaller than we expected and a bit worn-looking. A queen-size bed took up most of the floor space. There was a small television with a DVD player, a dresser and mirror, a single upholstered chair, and a freestanding electric fireplace. Two robes hung in a doorless closet. In fairness, several other rooms we peeked into on Sunday morning were more up-to-date and attractively decorated. The best part of our room was the bath, dominated by an oversized whirlpool tub. ❖ Breakfast was served at individual tables set with linen tablecloths and napkins and Wedgwood china. On Saturday, we had a choice of blueberry or chocolate chip pancakes with bacon, and on Sunday we enjoyed eggs Florentine with ham, along with juice, fresh fruit, yogurt, and granola. ❖ The Gerraughtys were consummate hosts, from David's insistence on carrying our bags up the stairs on Friday evening to Seely's frequent queries about whether we wanted more of anything at breakfast. ❖ In addition to eight guest rooms, the inn has a two-bedroom apartment (rented weekly in the summer; children allowed). Best of all, a summer rental includes beach passes for everyone.

ELLEN ALBANESE, *Globe Staff*

Sturbridge Country Inn

Getaway 13

530 Main St.,
Sturbridge, Mass.
508-347-5503
www.sturbridgecountryinn.com

RATES
15 rooms. $99-$189.

WHAT WE LIKED MOST
Finding both a fireplace and a whirlpool tub in a moderately priced room.

WHAT WE LIKED LEAST
Fake fig trees and dusty fabric floral arrangements.

WHAT SURPRISED US
A large, heated outdoor pool.

YOU KNOW YOU'RE AT STURBRIDGE COUNTRY INN WHEN... *peaked ceilings and exposed beams in nearly every room attest to the building's 1840s heritage.*

THINGS TO REMEMBER
_____
_____
_____
_____

MAINE • NEW HAMPSHIRE • VERMONT • **MASS**

WE LOVE OLD NEW ENGLAND INNS with wide floorboards, exposed-beam ceilings, and fireplaces. We are also partial to whirlpool tubs. ❖ The Sturbridge Country Inn seems designed to win the hearts of travelers like us. Every room in this 15-room hostelry dating from the 1840s includes a fireplace and whirlpool, and a heated outdoor pool is open from May to September. ❖ The post-and-beam structure with a classic Victorian Greek Revival facade is centrally located on Main Street, also Route 20. There are shops and restaurants within walking distance, and Sturbridge Village is half a mile away. On a Friday night we received a warm welcome from the young woman at the front desk. She showed us around the inn's rustic lobby, with its rough-hewn beams, fireplace, and built-in bookcases, and even cranked up an old phonograph to prove it still worked. ❖ Our spacious "corner deluxe room" on the second floor felt even larger because of the vaulted ceiling. There was a king-size bed with a nightstand on one side and a low dresser on the other. A small television sat atop a mini refrigerator. An alcove held a table and two chairs, with a coffeemaker and hanging lamp. The whirlpool tub occupied one corner of the room and linked the sleeping area to the bathroom. From the bedroom, the deep green tub was hidden by black and pale green sheers; it was separated from the bathroom by frosted glass shower doors. A pretty basket of white towels sat on a marble step that made it easy to get in and out. We were sorry the gas fireplace wasn't visible from the whirlpool. ❖ The bathroom was roomy with plenty of storage space, bright lights on both sides of the mirror, a hair dryer, heat lamp, and fan. ❖ Despite the inn's downtown location, we were not bothered by street noise. And despite the building's age, we heard not a peep from neighboring rooms, though most were occupied on the second night of our stay. ❖ Attached to the main building is a restored barn with additional rooms. Until 2005 the barn also housed a restaurant, but that space has been given over to two more deluxe rooms that have decks overlooking the pool, as well as fireplaces and whirlpools. ❖ Continental breakfast served in the lobby included cereal, granola, fruit, yogurt, mini-bagels, English muffins, sweet muffins, orange juice, and coffee. Guests can eat at tables in the lobby or take breakfast back to their rooms.

ELLEN ALBANESE, *Globe Staff*

Chatham Wayside Inn

Getaway 14

512 Main St.,
Chatham, Mass.
800-242-8426 or 508-945-5550
www.waysideinn.com

RATES
56 rooms. $110-$425.

WHAT WE LIKED MOST
Friendly and helpful staff.

WHAT WE LIKED LEAST
The $3-a-night energy surcharge, imposed starting in 2005.

WHAT SURPRISED US
The modesty of the continental breakfast.

YOU KNOW YOU'RE AT CHATHAM WAYSIDE INN WHEN ... *the action of the village swirls all around your isle of tranquility.*

THINGS TO REMEMBER
_____
_____
_____
_____

THE DESK CLERK BUBBLED with enthusiasm when we checked into the Chatham Wayside Inn. "We're here 24 hours a day, if you need anything," she said, handing us each a key attached to a big brass tag. "We set out coffee and tea at 6:30 in the morning if you can't wait until breakfast begins at 8. Oh, and there's a computer for guests in case you need to check your e-mail." ❖ The e-mail station is a rare nod to modernity at an inn that remains a study in traditional styling and understated good taste. Although structures have been added over the years, the property began life as a private home in 1860 and began functioning as a hostelry not long after. The sprawling inn still dominates the crest of Main Street, right next to Kate Gould Park, site of Friday-night band concerts in summer. ❖ Our room, No. 201, was up a half flight of steps in the main inn. The main sitting and sleeping area featured three windows, one with a view of Main Street and two on a side that looked out, alas, onto the parking lot rather than the park. The soothing decor seemed inspired by a country garden, with its deep blue carpet and cornflower blue coverlet with red, pink, and green floral pattern. Two diminutive wing chairs in a subtle red geometric pattern flanked a small table with a shiny brass lamp. ❖ From the inn, it didn't take long to stroll the length of Main Street, checking out the few gift shops, galleries, clothing stores, bookshop, and candy store open on a Friday afternoon in late March. Then we drove to ever-shifting South Beach to join dog walkers and shell collectors as the sky started to turn rosy for sunset. ❖ Since the inn's bar and dining room were closed for renovations during our visit, we picked the nearby "sister property," Christian's Restaurant, for dinner. Every dish on the menu was named for a Hollywood movie, never a good omen. But sticking to local scallops and quahogs proved wise, and the convivial room and upbeat service made up for any kitchen shortcomings. A coconut-chocolate bread pudding delivered a tasty conclusion. ❖ On the walk back to our room, loud oldies rock poured from the Chatham Squire restaurant. We wondered if the music might drift in those street-facing windows, but as old-fashioned as they looked, they were double-pane sealed against weather and noise. The serene illusion of Olde Cape Cod was intact.

PATRICIA HARRIS AND DAVID LYON, *Globe Correspondents*

Watson House

Getaway 15

1876 Main St.,
South Windsor, Conn.
860-282-8888
www.thewatsonhouse.com

RATES
Five rooms. $99-$189.

WHAT WE LIKED MOST
Our meltingly soft bed with 400-thread count bedding.

WHAT WE LIKED LEAST
The cavernous inn's occasional feeling of emptiness.

WHAT SURPRISED US
The size of this 21-room, 13-fireplace mansion.

YOU KNOW YOU'RE AT WATSON HOUSE WHEN... you walk in and feel swallowed by the wide, high-ceilinged main hall on the first floor.

THINGS TO REMEMBER
_____
_____
_____
_____
_____

MAINE • NEW HAMPSHIRE • VERMONT • MASS

"**HELLO?**" Silence. "Hello?" More silence. We called out again, this time louder. "Hello? Is anyone home?" But all we heard was the sound of our voices drifting through the cavernous room we had entered. It was less a room than a massive hall that stretched the length of the house, from front door to back, and felt disconcertingly vast and hollow. ❖ That feeling would mark our stay at the Watson House, a three-story mansion built for a local merchant, John Watson, in 1788. Do the math: This imposing, impressively preserved structure, located in South Windsor's historic district a short walk from the Connecticut River, is 220 years old. ❖ That makes it a fascinating relic, and explains why it is opened for public tours during the local historical society's annual "heritage day." But that same architectural grandeur can be a handicap for a bed-and-breakfast. How, after all, do you make a mansion with 21 rooms and 13 fireplaces cozy? That is the challenge for Brandy and Mike Feldmeier, a young couple who turned Watson House into a five-bedroom inn last year. ❖ By their account, the house needed cosmetic help when they bought it. They ditched most of the furnishings and replaced them with pieces that match the mansion's post-Revolutionary War style. ❖ Our spacious, second-floor bedroom, called the Adams Suite, had a reproduction bedroom set whose centerpiece was a gorgeous, king-sized, four-post mahogany bed with 400-thread count bedding. I have always considered the hoopla over thread count silly, but this meltingly soft bed was the most comfortable I have slept in. Other good things about our room: the remote-controlled gas fireplace, private bathroom with shower, and windows overlooking a field of sheep. ❖ This is where I should mention that a month after the Feldmeiers bought the inn, Brandy began to feel a touch nauseated. The queasiness was morning sickness. In November 2006, daughter Hayden was born — she is named after the house's architect, Thomas Hayden — and Brandy and Mike's lives have been hectic ever since. ❖ Hayden's arrival meant they had to slow down the redecorating and focus their time and expenses on their baby. That's why Watson House remains a work in progress, and why we were willing to forgive its rough spots. ❖ We wouldn't change a thing about breakfast, though. Brandy is the cook, and guests choose from a menu that can include eggs, omelets, quiche, pancakes, sticky buns, fresh fruit, and, our favorite, Belgian waffles made with cinnamon-buttermilk batter. Topped with blueberries and strawberries, they make a perfect meal.

SACHA PFEIFFER, *Globe Staff*

Mowry-Nicholson House

Getaway 16

*57 Brownell St.,
Providence, R.I.
401-351-6111
www.providence-suites.com*

RATES
12 rooms. $129-$250.

WHAT WE LIKED MOST
The graciousness of our hosts.

WHAT WE LIKED LEAST
The lack of space in our room.

WHAT SURPRISED US
The many amenities. Who uses a phone in the bathroom, anyway?

YOU KNOW YOU'RE AT THE MOWRY-NICHOLSON HOUSE WHEN... *Piper, the cockatiel, chirps a welcome.*

THINGS TO REMEMBER

IT WAS A SPECTACULAR VIEW, the marble Rhode Island State House glowing pale in the black night, so close it seemed to loom above our dinner table. Just one more thing the innkeeper had arranged for us? ❖ Earlier in the day, she had listened sympathetically to our tale of the previous night's fitful dinner, when our toddler made clear his desire to leave a downtown restaurant long before the appetizers arrived. So when we decided to surrender to takeout the second night of our stay, she encouraged us to eat at the inn's dining room table. ❖ The Mowry-Nicholson House serves only breakfast, so the dining room was quiet when we arrived, steaming cardboard containers in hand. Lights dimmed, the scene was a vision in elegance: Cloth napkins and placemats had been arranged at our seats, facing the window and the stunning dome. It was hard to remember that not long ago this grand Victorian mansion, shuttered and crumbling, nearly became a parking lot. The house, named for its two earliest owners, was built in 1856. But it was later broken up into apartments, and then, a boarding house. As the 21st century dawned, the house was abandoned and the group that owned the property planned to tear it down. ❖ Instead, Phyllis and Ken Parker bought the building. The Parkers had owned inns on Nantucket, including the Tuckernuck Inn, for a quarter-century and thought they were beginning retirement. Instead, they found themselves in Providence, running the Mowry-Nicholson House and, a block away, its sister inn, the Christopher Dodge House. They restored both, which are listed on the National Register of Historic Places. Both inns lie along Smith Hill, not far from downtown. ❖ The main bedroom in our second-floor room was a bit cramped, with a king-size bed filling most of the room. But the rooms are filled with conveniences: wireless Internet, a television in both the sitting room and the bedroom, two phones, including one in the bathroom, and a personalized heating system that includes overhead heating/cooling fans. ❖ Breakfast was served each morning in the brick dining room of the Dodge House, an Italianate mansion whose rooms have high ceilings and wide-board wooden floors. It's the more elegant and spacious of the two inns, although only the Mowry-Nicholson House has two-room suites. The breakfast was extensive: a wonderful brie omelet the first day, and a buffet packed with bagels, fruit, yogurt, pastries, fruit salad, and cereal. The second day was disappointing, though: a thick slice of baked apple cake that was more mushy than decadent.

KATHLEEN BURGE, *Globe Staff*
RICH BARLOW, *Globe Correspondent*

Hotel Commonwealth

Getaway 17

500 Commonwealth Ave.,
Boston, Mass.
617-933-5000 or 866-784-4000
www.hotelcommonwealth.com

RATES
150 rooms. $245-$485.

WHAT WE LIKED MOST
The way the hotel shut out the clamor of Kenmore Square.

WHAT WE LIKED LEAST
The lack of an early coffee option in the gallery of shops; Truly Jorg's Patisserie was only slowly perking up at 8 a.m.

WHAT SURPRISED US
The size of our room, about one-third larger than the Boston average.

YOU KNOW YOU'RE AT HOTEL COMMONWEALTH WHEN... *your room is bookended by restaurants, one upscale (Great Bay) and one casual (Eastern Standard).*

THINGS TO REMEMBER

MAINE • NEW HAMPSHIRE • VERMONT • MASS

WHEN THE RED SOX ANNOUNCED that they had signed pitcher Daisuke Matsuzaka in late 2006, the Hotel Commonwealth leaped on the news like a batter eyeing a gyroball that's not … um, gyrating. The hotel made much of its website available in Japanese in a bid to steer the influx of visitors hoping to see the superstar from Japan's Pacific League. Judging by what the hotel has managed in less than four years, we expected the equivalent of an inside-the-park home run. ❖ We stayed there on a frigid February night before pitchers and catchers had even reported, and we were happy to step out of the car onto a curbside check-in area warmed by blowers in the awning above. The sense of comfort was heightened by the almost eerie quiet that descended when the door closed on bustling Kenmore Square. ❖ The award-winning hotel had its genesis in the mid-1990s, when Terrence Guiney and a group of partners were doing some real estate consulting for Boston University. Guiney, the hotel's managing director, saw a logical client base, with BU, Simmons and Emmanuel colleges, and a big medical complex several blocks up Brookline Avenue. ❖ From the lobby, with its understatedly elegant pieces and circular divan begging to be sprawled upon, it was easy to negotiate the 150-room building, which has a dozen or so shops on the lobby level. Its rooms are labeled either Fenway or Commonwealth: Fenway rooms, a tad smaller at 470 square feet, face the rear with a view of the stadium across the Mass. Pike. Commonwealth rooms face the square and are 515 square feet. (Guiney said a typical room in the city is 350 square feet.) We were impressed with the spaciousness of our Fenway room, not to mention its view of the rear of the ballpark's center-field message board, which made the chill recede a bit more. ❖ The room's walls were a pale yellow and white, an almost sponged look that turned to stripes in the bathroom. Italian linens and Egyptian cotton blankets were complemented by a rust-colored throw across the bottom of the bed. The room's period furniture was distinctive, with a striking armoire holding the TV/DVD player, a minibar, and some drawers. The pieces, said Guiney, "are all one-of-a-kind, designed here and made in Oman in the Persian Gulf. You're not going to walk into another hotel and find them." ❖ Another nice touch was the room information book, packaged to look like a leather-bound volume you might find at Commonwealth Books, an antiquarian bookshop in the retail gallery.

RON DRISCOLL, *Globe Staff*

Riverbend Inn Bed & Breakfast

Getaway 18

273 Chocorua Mountain Highway, Chocorua, N.H.
603-323-7440 or 800-628-6944
www.riverbendinn.com

RATES
10 rooms. $100-$235.

WHAT WE LIKED MOST
The seamless melding of Western architecture and Eastern decor.

WHAT WE LIKED LEAST
The fact that there was only one chair in our room.

WHAT SURPRISED US
The lavish and beautifully presented breakfasts.

YOU KNOW YOU'RE AT THE RIVERBEND INN WHEN... *from nearly any spot you can see and hear the bubbling Chocorua River.*

THINGS TO REMEMBER

MAINE • **NEW HAMPSHIRE** • VERMONT • MASS

RARELY HAVE I FELT AS SERENE as I did sitting on the red velvet cushion of a window seat at the Riverbend Inn Bed & Breakfast in late March, watching the Chocorua River burble its way between snow-covered banks until the foamy copper ribbon disappeared around a forested bend. ❖ Perhaps it was the massage still radiating warmth across my shoulders. Perhaps it was Sinatra on the sound system. Perhaps it was the lushly decorated parlor that combines brick-red walls, a wood-burning fireplace, and striking Asian accents such as a golden six-foot statue of Dwarapalaka, the Hindu god of entryways, and richly hued silk shawls tossed across the couches. ❖ Innkeepers Craig Cox and Jerry Weiss have created a surprisingly seamless melding of East and West, filled with treasures they have collected traveling and enriched by their family histories. Ask just one question about the decor and you quickly learn that every object has a story. ❖ The sprawling inn set on 15 acres comprises two buildings, connected by a breakfast room. Windows on both sides bring the outside in, and in warm weather breakfast is served on a deck overlooking the river, which fills the air with its soft rushing sound. ❖ We were struck by the bold use of color in our room on the second floor. Walls and ceiling were painted the same olive green, broken only by a thin strip of white molding around the top of the room. Sage green drapes framed the windows and a jacquard spread covered the king-size bed, with a decorative mahogany headboard. The L-shaped room also held a wood armoire and a single upholstered chair in green velvet, next to a floor lamp. The monochromatic effect was soothing. ❖ Nearly all the rooms use the same monochromatic color scheme, in such vibrant hues as Chinese red and aubergine. The breakfast room, on the other hand, is a sea of white (walls, tables and chairs, linens, ceramic dishes) accented by a red brick floor and green plants. Even Weiss glides in and out to serve wearing chef's whites and sandals. ❖ Cox's breakfasts are creative and beautifully presented. A fruit parfait layered fresh berries and yogurt, topped with granola; it was followed by pancakes with bacon and maple syrup. A fruit garnish of green grapes, cantaloupe, and strawberries was clearly chosen for its contrast of shapes and colors as well as taste. Sunday morning brought poached pears and an egg casserole with mushrooms and leeks. Guests help themselves to coffee, juice, and local apple cider.

ELLEN ALBANESE, *Globe Staff*

General Stanton Inn

Getaway 19

4115 Old Post Road,
Charlestown, R.I.
800-364-8011 or 401-364-8888
www.generalstantoninn.com

RATES
15 rooms. $75-$300.

WHAT WE LIKED MOST
The friendly, accommodating staff.

WHAT WE LIKED LEAST
The lack of soundproofing.

WHAT SURPRISED US
The small price differential between a motel-style small room and one of the nicer historic rooms.

YOU KNOW YOU'RE AT GENERAL STANTON INN WHEN... *the driveway snakes past a field of plots for flea-market vendors.*

THINGS TO REMEMBER

SET ON SEVERAL ACRES on the Old Post Road near Charlestown Beach, the General Stanton Inn hosts a popular weekend flea market. When the season opened in April, we booked a Friday night at the inn to catch the next day's early-bird bargains. The inn is an oddity among old New England buildings in that the first structure — a house moved to the site in 1667 and now known as the Indian Room — forms the core of the building rather than the front. The main house, which includes the largest of the dining rooms, dates from 1740. ❖ We had to walk outdoors to reach Room 11, one of six on the back of the building with individual entrances along a covered porch. Though clean and fresh, the motel-like character was a letdown after the beamed ceilings of the dining rooms and rusticity of the tavern. A queen bed with dark wood headboard and posts took half the floor space. Two green velour wing chairs flanked a small table and lamp by the window, and another lamp glowed from a low dresser. ❖ The Night Watch Tavern, with its rough wood walls and massive stone fireplace, seemed like the best bet for dinner, and the food transcended conventional pub grub. By the time we finished, the band was ready to start playing in the tavern. Alas, our room reverberated with the sound of the band, which was scheduled to play until 1 a.m. ❖ When we returned to the office to ask about a quieter room, the desk clerk could not have been more apologetic or accommodating, finally offering the Block Island room on the second floor in the main building. "It's our nicest," she said. ❖ Dramatic wallpaper of pink and green flora on a black background covered two walls (the other two were a subtler pink). An impressive cannonball post bed stood between two matching night tables with tall white ceramic lamps. The faint music was mere background noise, though the strumming and drumming seemed louder when we turned off the TV in our room. Fortunately, the air conditioning unit's fan masked the noise so we could enjoy a comfortable night's sleep. Visions of flea market finds danced in our heads. ❖ Saturday dawned overcast, and we planned to have breakfast as the dealers set up their wares. But the tavern and office were locked up tight. We learned later that breakfast service would begin in mid-May. At 8:30 a.m., the General Stanton still stood dark and mute, perhaps sleeping in from the merriment of the night before.

PATRICIA HARRIS AND DAVID LYON, *Globe Correspondents*

Victoria Inn

Getaway 20

430 High St.,
Hampton, N.H.
603-929-1437 or 800-291-2672
www.thevictoriainn.com

RATES
Six rooms. $100-$150.

WHAT WE LIKED MOST
Innkeeper John Nyhan's unflappable hospitality.

WHAT WE LIKED LEAST
Our fair-to-middling breakfast.

WHAT SURPRISED US
That such pretty, peaceful lodging can be found so close to honky-tonk Hampton Beach.

YOU KNOW YOU'RE AT THE VICTORIA INN WHEN... the gregarious Nyhan greets you at the front door with a firm handshake and hearty hello.

THINGS TO REMEMBER

THE MOTHER OF THE BRIDE had an emergency. Her daughter was scheduled to get married on Hampton Beach in late April — just a few days away — and the weather was atrocious. The woman, frantic, phoned John Nyhan with a question: Could he help? ❖ He could. In less than a week, Nyhan, who with his wife, Pamela, owns the Victoria Inn, a bed-and-breakfast not far from the beach, arranged a simple wedding at the inn for about 25 people. He ordered flowers, decorated an outdoor gazebo for the ceremony, and planned a front porch champagne toast. Crisis averted, the bride and groom got married without a hitch. ❖ But what impressed me most about that 11th-hour rescue, which took place when we visited the Victoria Inn, was Nyhan's unflappable hospitality in the midst of such madness. ❖ The wedding was held on a Saturday morning, and we were the inn's only guests on Friday night. Nyhan was clearly busy with final arrangements, but we never felt slighted in the least. There's a reason Nyhan is a pro at party planning: The Victoria Inn hosts about 80 private functions a year, from weddings to bridal and baby showers to birthday, anniversary, and retirement parties. He helps arrange caterers, florists, photographers, and other vendors, and he lets guests customize their parties however they like. ❖ The inn's decor tends to be traditional bed-and-breakfast, meaning lots of floral patterns, lace curtains, fringed lamp shades, and period antiques. It's not suffocating, though. Our spacious bedroom, called the honeymoon suite, had a four-poster king-size bed, sitting area with two chairs and a coffee table, and windowed sunporch with an antique chaise and slightly worn couch. The porch was a nice, warm spot for reading, and we loved the natural light that streamed through it. As we fell asleep, we could hear frogs peeping in the night. ❖ Because our room faced the street, we also occasionally heard the whoosh of passing traffic. The noise wasn't too bad, at least in mid-April. But if I were to go back I'd ask for a room near the back, just to be safe. The inn's location is ideal — about a half-mile from Hampton Beach in one direction, about 2 miles from downtown Hampton in the other. ❖ Nyhan's an uneven cook, but so warm and hospitable that I'm willing to cut him some slack. I might not hire him as a chef, but if I ever need a last-minute wedding, he would be my first call.

SACHA PFEIFFER, *Globe Staff*

The Inn at Ormsby Hill

Getaway 21

*1842 Main St.,
Manchester, Vt.
802-362-1163 or 800-670-2841
www.ormsbyhill.com*

RATES
10 rooms. $195-$435.

WHAT WE LIKED MOST
The bathroom suite was almost like having your own private water amusement park.

WHAT WE LIKED LEAST
The thin bed pillows and the water stains on the Tower's bedchamber ceiling.

WHAT SURPRISED US
That this plush and lavish inn was an abandoned building waiting to be razed in the 1980s.

YOU KNOW YOU'RE AT THE INN AT ORMSBY HILL WHEN... it's impossible to look out any window without taking in delicious mountain vistas.

THINGS TO REMEMBER

MAINE · NEW HAMPSHIRE · *VERMONT* · MASS

THE TOWN OF MANCHESTER, not far from the New York border, is the Green Mountain State's answer to Freeport, Maine. It's chock-full of outlet stores, but instead of a nearby ocean, you get mountain views. ❖ Overnight visitors seeking a unique Manchester experience usually flock to the Equinox Resort. But sometimes you crave just a quiet little getaway, a place with a cozy, informal atmosphere ... and your own tower. ❖ The Inn at Ormsby Hill has 10 rooms, each with a distinctive personality — and one of them is in a tower. The Tower is actually a mini-suite on three levels, and the top floor offers the kind of diversions that make you want to hang a "Do Not Disturb" sign on the door. ❖ The Tower's third floor is an oversized bathroom. It includes windows with astounding mountain views, a two-person Jacuzzi, and an oversized shower stall with a bench and showerheads on opposite walls. Click a couple of buttons, and it begins its conversion into a steam sauna. ❖ Owners Ted and Chris Sprague realized the bathroom would be the Tower's centerpiece, so they've filled it with a variety of items, both practical and whimsical, that enliven the experience. There are candles and potpourri as well as items ranging from bath salts and Aveda products to energy bars. ❖ The Tower's main living space has its allure, with a flat-screen television, gas fireplace, a sitting area with sofa and wing chair, and a queen-size maple canopy bed. Each room has its own charms. Some have refrigerators, and others have more impressive amenities. But there is only one Tower. ❖ The inn's main building is one of the oldest in Manchester and was erected in 1764. Ask for a tour of the premises and Ted Sprague just might take you down to the basement and show you an old jail cell, with rusty bars intact. Was it once used as a local prison? No one is certain. Just as no one is sure whether the Revolutionary War hero Ethan Allen did, indeed, hide out at the inn or if it once served as a safe house for the Underground Railroad. ❖ Meals are served in the Conservatory, one of several common rooms. It's large and impressive with a startling fireplace and plenty of natural light. It's also where you'll find complimentary sherry and snacks each afternoon. ❖ Our three-course breakfast featured espresso coffeecake, bananas and hot toasted almonds in cream, and ridiculously light and fluffy scrambled eggs in a croissant. By meal's end, we were well fueled for the outlet wars.

DEAN JOHNSON, *Globe Correspondent*

Point Independence Inn

Getaway 22

9 Eagle Way,
Onset, Mass.
508-273-0466 or 866-827-4466
www.pointindependenceinn.com

RATES
Six rooms. $129-$279.

WHAT WE LIKED MOST
The spare, thoughtful decor that lets the setting's natural beauty take center stage.

WHAT WE LIKED LEAST
The small bath with the sink in the room and no storage space.

WHAT SURPRISED US
The lack of breakfast service during the offseason.

YOU KNOW YOU'RE AT THE POINT INDEPENDENCE INN WHEN... *you look onto expanses of water and sand from nearly every room.*

THINGS TO REMEMBER
_____
_____
_____
_____
_____

MAINE • NEW HAMPSHIRE • VERMONT • **MASS**

WITH A SETTING THIS SPECTACULAR — at the intersection of the East River, Onset Bay, and the Cape Cod Canal — an inn might get away with offering nothing more than the natural beauty of sea and sand. Happily, the Point Independence Inn offers more: cordial hosts, pleasing decor, comfortable rooms, and a spa. Having missed the exit off Route 25, we drove the streets of Wareham until we saw the cream-colored stucco building, with turrets and a striking red clay tile roof, looming at the land's end. ❖ The decor is Mediterranean-mansion-meets-Tommy-Bahama, starting with a parking lot of shimmering white crushed shells. Inside, natural colors predominate: beige and brown walls, grass cloth in the parlor, and gleaming hardwood floors. On the first floor, spacious windows open onto a panorama of sand and sea; the distinction between indoors and outdoors is almost transparent. In summer guests can rent kayaks to paddle Onset Bay, by Wicket and Onset islands. The inn will also make reservations for charter fishing trips. ❖ Michael and Jackie Kennedy bought the inn, which dates to 1880, at auction five years ago and closed it for a year for a complete overhaul. They excised all things Victorian and floral, replacing them with natural woods, neutral colors, and tropical accents. ❖ We stayed in the Harbor View Room, the inn's second-largest accommodation. The spacious room has an extruded round sitting area with three deep windows. Olive sheer curtains with gold embroidery keep the lovely view in focus, and wood slat blinds provide privacy. There were two comfortable cushioned wicker chairs in the alcove, a bright and pleasant place in the daylight, but it was impossible to read after dark, since there were no lamps by the chairs. ❖ The queen bed had an intricately carved headboard and posts. Two rattan and leather narrow chests served as night tables. A lovely floral lacquered chest and a gold-colored pedestal fan added to the Casablanca feel. There was a large sink in the room and a small bath with a toilet and shower. ❖ We took advantage of a "two by the sea" couples massage, simultaneous treatments in adjoining rooms. The spa was attractive and soothing. Coffee and tea are available 24 hours a day, but we were surprised to find that breakfast is not served in the off-season. On a Sunday morning in April, we faced a tough decision: Stay and savor the inn's spectacular setting until checkout or head for the local diner? We chose to defer breakfast for one last walk on the beach.

ELLEN ALBANESE, *Globe Staff*

Governor Bradford House
Country Inn

Getaway 23

250 Metacom Ave. (Mount Hope Farm),
Bristol, R.I.
877-254-9300, 401-254-9300
www.mounthopefarm.com

RATES
11 rooms. $175-$225.

WHAT WE LIKED MOST
Feeling like lords of the manor.

WHAT WE LIKED LEAST
That the weather was too warm to light a fire in our fireplace.

WHAT SURPRISED US
That the loud chimes of the grandfather clock on the first floor didn't disturb us once we closed the two doors to our room.

YOU KNOW YOU'RE AT THE GOVERNOR BRADFORD HOUSE WHEN ... both red and white Rhode Island roosters start crowing at first light.

THINGS TO REMEMBER

JOHN PAUL SMITH KNOWS the ins and outs of this old house. "Watch your head," he warned, pointing to the low overhang as we climbed the front stairway. When we passed through a short doorway into the vestibule of our room, he said it again: "Watch your head." He chuckled. "In general," he added, "just watch your head. And when you go to take a shower, turn on the hot water and go do something else while it warms up. This is an old house, after all." ❖ The front portion of the Governor Bradford House was built in 1745 as a summer home for Isaac Royall, a Loyalist who fled to Nova Scotia on the eve of the Revolution. Located on a vast tract of farmland between Narragansett and Mount Hope bays, the house is generally associated with William Bradford, who bought the 2½-story brick-ender in 1783. Our room, Number 2, was named for Rudolf F. Haffenreffer Jr., a collector of Native American artifacts who acquired Mount Hope Farm in 1916 and, after the repeal of Prohibition, built on his family's brewing heritage at Narragansett brewery. ❖ From the vestibule, two short steps led into a broad room where light flooded in through four 12-over-12 windows. Opposite the king-size four-poster bed, a working fireplace was laid with a Duraflame log. "Be sure to take the room key with you when you go out," said Smith, director of sales and marketing for the Mount Hope Trust, which acquired the property in 1999. The key would also open the inn door, which he would lock when he left at 5 p.m. (A caretaker lives right across the driveway.) Smith encouraged us to follow the 1½-mile paved road that winds through the property to the shores of Mount Hope Bay. ❖ The road, lined with stone walls meticulously laid by the Works Progress Administration during the Depression, winds through the 200 acres that remain of Haffenreffer's 550-acre saltwater dairy farm. A handful of milk cows and a few shaggy Scottish Highland cattle grazed under trees, and pheasants and chickens cackled and screeched from their pens. ❖ We were safely indoors before a storm front darkened the sky. We settled down to read in the first-floor music room, with its baby grand piano, comfortable chairs and couch, fireplace, and wall-sized window that looked across the grounds to the water. Next morning, Vicky White had laid out warm blueberry muffins, yogurt, fruit, and juice, coffee, and tea. And dueling roosters had signaled that the property still runs on farm time.

PATRICIA HARRIS AND DAVID LYON, *Globe Correspondents*

The Golden Slipper

Getaway 24

Lewis Wharf,
Boston, Mass.
781-545-2845
www.bostonsbedandbreakfastafloat.com

RATES
$185; open May 1-Nov. 15.

WHAT WE LIKED MOST
The location. Lewis Wharf is within easy walking distance of the North End, Quincy Market, and Faneuil Hall.

WHAT WE LIKED LEAST
The prepackaged breakfast-in-a-basket.

WHAT SURPRISED US
How much the boat moves while moored at the dock.

YOU KNOW YOU'RE AT THE GOLDEN SLIPPER WHEN... you hear water lapping the hull and watch the boats of Boston Harbor while relaxing on the outside deck.

THINGS TO REMEMBER

MAINE · NEW HAMPSHIRE · VERMONT · MASS

WHAT WAS I THINKING? How could a landlubber like myself — one whose entire nautical vocabulary consists of "Ahoy matey!" — possibly book a two-night stay at a bed-and-breakfast on a boat? How could I forget that I get seasick and I'm claustrophobic? ❖ I could and I did, blithely reserving two nights on the Golden Slipper, a "B&B Afloat" on Lewis Wharf in Boston Harbor. Excluding my personal challenges, it was a delightful experience. ❖ On a warm holiday weekend, owner Gretchen Stephenson greeted us at the dock and gave us a tour of the 1960 Chris Craft that she bought, gutted, and renovated as a bed-and-breakfast in 1991. ❖ "You can experience the novelty of living on a boat without having to buy it and maintain it," said Stephenson. ❖ We learned how to refill the water tank (if necessary), where to find a flashlight, and how to correctly use the head. We located outlets for the fans, toured the galley (microwave and toaster), received instructions for operating the TV, and were shown a small cache of videos and DVDs available to watch. Then Stephenson shook hands farewell and we were on our own. ❖ The boat has three living areas (four if you count the aft deck with faux-wicker furniture) decorated like a Victorian guesthouse, complete with pink floral wallpaper, bedding, and slipcovers; white lace tablecloths and curtains; painted china cups, and knickknacks galore. ❖ The central space, a combination living and dining room (with four pink dining chairs), is light-filled and open. A double futon couch can accommodate two more overnight guests, presumably friends you wouldn't mind sharing close quarters with. ❖ The aft bedroom, down a few steps, has a double bed, closet for storing bags, modest shower (with a pink bejeweled curtain), and head that's stocked with an assortment of small bottles of shampoo, conditioner, and body gel. At night, the rocking motion ceased as harbor traffic subsided, so sleeping was not a problem. ❖ Our favorite spot was the rear deck, where we enjoyed the salty breezes and watched the parade of vessels in the harbor. We preferred the quiet of early morning to the sounds of late-night revelers jammed on the deck of a nearby restaurant and bar. ❖ With no real cooking facilities onboard, we strolled to Hanover Street and had a memorable dinner at Bricco. The waiter brought the check and asked if we had valet-parked our car. "No," we said, "we're walking — back to our boat." ❖ For that brief moment we lived the fantasy of the Golden Slipper: We were boaters. Ahoy matey!

NECEE REGIS, *Globe Correspondent*

The Inn on Peaks Island

Getaway 25

33 Island Ave.,
Peaks Island, Maine
207-766-5100
www.innonpeaks.com

RATES
Six rooms. Varies seasonally, $175-$300.

WHAT WE LIKED MOST
The sleepy quality of the island combined with the friendly inn staff created a stress-free vacation.

WHAT WE LIKED LEAST
The lack of a screen door to the outside deck meant flies and mosquitoes could enter with the cool bay breezes.

WHAT SURPRISED US
The building looks like a renovated older house, but it was built five years ago.

YOU KNOW YOU'RE AT THE INN ON PEAKS ISLAND WHEN... you can watch from your deck as the Casco Bay Lines ferry arrives almost every hour from Portland.

THINGS TO REMEMBER

MAINE • NEW HAMPSHIRE • VERMONT • MASS

ON THE CUSP OF JUNE, I disembarked from the too-brief ferry ride from Portland and was greeted by the scent of lilacs mingling with the salt-tinged air of Casco Bay. Lilacs! Long after Boston's blooms had faded, bushes here were in full flower, creating the sensation that I had stepped back in time. ❖ It's easy to feel this way on Peaks Island, 2 miles long and 1 mile across, where the year-round population is 800. Sidewalks are few, yards sport tire swings, and cottages wear nametags like "Pinehurst" and "West O' The Moon." ❖ The easygoing, small-town feel continued at The Inn on Peaks Island. The staff was friendly and helpful whether I was searching for the cable TV lineup or getting plates from the dining room for an impromptu picnic on my deck overlooking the harbor. ❖ It's a short walk from the ferry up to the inn, which has the appearance of a well-restored property from the early 20th century, but surprisingly is only five years old. ❖ The inn describes its six rooms as "cottage-style," which in my room, the Chebeague Island Suite, meant simple, brightly colored, boxy furniture like a coral armoire (which hid the TV and DVD player), sea foam green dresser and side table, and plaid couch with many pillows. Wall-to-wall sisal carpet was nice underfoot, and a knotty pine cathedral ceiling opened up the sitting area where, in cooler weather, you can bask in the glow of a gas fireplace. An extra vanity outside the bathroom was a nice detail and the whirlpool tub was perfect for swirling stress away. ❖ Dining selections on the island are limited, but there's a restaurant open for lunch and dinner at the inn. The pub-style food was decent, the staff was cheerful, and the price was right. ❖ For breakfast off-season, there's the nearby Peaks Café, a colorful place where ferry-riders and locals gather for coffee, pastry, egg sandwiches, and breakfast burritos. Continental breakfast, served at the hotel during high season, was not available during my stay. ❖ After breakfast, it's an easy stroll to Brad's Recycled Bike Shop, where the rental department is self-serve: Pick out a bike and pay when you return. It takes less than an hour to circumnavigate the island at a leisurely pace. ❖ All roads eventually lead back to the landing and the inn, where the less ambitious can prop themselves on the deck and enjoy the glittering lights of Portland across the bay. And with not much more effort, you may imagine you've slipped back in time.

NECEE REGIS, *Globe Correspondent*

Seacrest Manor

Getaway 26

99 Marmion Way,
Rockport, Mass.
978-546-2211
www.seacrestmanor.com

RATES
Eight rooms. Varies seasonally; doubles $98-$215.

WHAT WE LIKED MOST
The warm hospitality of the innkeeper and her staff.

WHAT WE LIKED LEAST
On a cool rainy weekend we would have loved to see fires crackling in the downstairs fireplaces.

WHAT SURPRISED US
The Old World elegance behind the traditional New England exterior.

YOU KNOW YOU'RE AT THE SEACREST MANOR WHEN... *you can see the twin lighthouses of Thacher Island from the parlor and end bedrooms.*

THINGS TO REMEMBER

MAINE · NEW HAMPSHIRE · VERMONT · MASS

SEEN FROM THE BALCONY OF SEACREST MANOR, the twin lighthouses of Thacher Island seem both warning and welcoming, simultaneously alerting vessels to the rocky shoals and suggesting that cozy lodging awaits on shore. A sailor would do well to navigate that rocky coastline to secure a berth at this boutique inn, which describes its setting as "overlooking woods and sea." The welcome was as warm as the weather was dreary when we checked in on a rainy spring weekend. The inn has been owned by innkeeper Pat Saville's family since 1973. ❖ The exterior of the center-entrance Colonial — weathered brown shingles, white trim, mustard yellow shutters — doesn't prepare a visitor for the elegant, English country manor interior. High ceilings and wide doorways create a spacious feel. Burgundy carpet, wallpaper in bold prints, and crystal chandeliers suggest a European setting. Oils in ornate gold frames adorn the walls, and fresh flowers from the inn's garden accent the decor. ❖ The house is a few hundred yards from the ocean on Marmion Way, a narrow, winding road about a mile from the town center, along which small inns and large homes are nearly indistinguishable from one another. Bow windows at one end of Seacrest Manor's parlor look out onto the twin lighthouses. Rooms 7 and 8 on the second floor afford this same lovely view, along with a private entrance to the sun deck. ❖ We stayed in Room 5, which was spacious, with floral wallpaper, deep windows overlooking the front lawn, and a nonworking fireplace. It had a king-size bed, dresser, two upholstered chairs, and a roomy closet. The bathroom was small but adequate and featured an item we wish we'd find everywhere: a plug-in nightlight. All we missed was a hair dryer. ❖ Saville has a talent for making guests comfortable. She offered umbrellas and recommended restaurants. When we returned from dinner, our bed was turned down and there were chocolates on the night table. ❖ Afternoon tea was set out in the parlor, with its big curved couch facing a bow window overlooking the sea. We poured tea from a silver pot into pretty china cups and savored lemon tea bread and frosted brownies. ❖ The sunny breakfast room overlooks the extensive gardens. We enjoyed fresh fruit, waffles, and bacon and eggs. Inn guests can walk to Old Garden Beach, less than a mile away, or bike or drive to other beaches or to Rockport Center. Or they can just relax on the sun deck, look out to Thacher Island and thank their lucky stars they arrived at Seacrest Manor by land.

ELLEN ALBANESE, *Globe Staff*

The Lighthouse Inn

Getaway 27

1 Lighthouse Inn Road,
West Dennis, Mass.
508-398-2244
www.lighthouseinn.com

RATES
68 rooms and cottages. Varies seasonally; $248-$322 for two.

WHAT WE LIKED MOST
Having both the privacy of our own cottage and the convenience of the nearby beach and restaurant.

WHAT WE LIKED LEAST
Getting spiked in the head by a piece of the lighthouse light.

WHAT SURPRISED US
That the heated pool was packed but the beach was nearly empty on a glorious summer day.

YOU KNOW YOU'RE AT THE LIGHTHOUSE INN WHEN... the light atop the main building flashes every six seconds.

THINGS TO REMEMBER

MAINE • NEW HAMPSHIRE • VERMONT • **MASS**

THERE COMES A TIME, early in parenthood, when you hear about an inn where the beach lies just beyond the clover-thick lawn. The restaurant along the water's edge serves both grilled salmon and peanut-butter-and-jelly sandwiches. High chairs abound. And you think: This must be paradise. ❖ No matter that you once considered yourself an adventurous traveler, stepping around poisonous snakes in the rain forest and hitchhiking through Eastern Europe. This is the new dream: jaunts to the beach that do not require struggles into a car seat; nap times where the crib is a minute's walk from the waves; dinners where you are not ostracized for the mountain of peas under your son's chair.
❖ And so our family of three recently spent a few blissfully relaxing days at the Lighthouse Inn, a cluster of 68 rooms and cottages along Nantucket Sound. The inn has been run by the Stone family since 1938. Although the lighthouse had been decommissioned in 1914, the Stones relighted it 17 years ago as the country's only privately owned working lighthouse.
As much as we enjoyed our stay, there was an occasional carelessness to detail. Still, many of the young staffers were hardworking, efficient, and earnest. ❖ The Lighthouse Inn sometimes feels like summer camp for adults because you keep bumping into the same guests at meals and on the beach. For those with older children, the inn offers parents precious adult time. The InnKids program, for ages 3 and up, ferries children to a day filled with arts and crafts and beach time. Parents can also drop off their kids to eat with other children and inn staffers during dinnertime. Despite the family focus, though, not everyone who stays at the inn brings children. We saw plenty of couples on their own, including one planning a wedding at the inn. ❖ We stayed in one of the Oceanview Cottages, a semicircle of shingled buildings on a small hill just behind the more expensive waterfront cottages. The difference in location is negligible; we still had a wide-open view of the waves from our front deck. Our cottage, with a working fireplace, air conditioning, and cable television, was simply but nicely furnished: two blue wingback chairs, a floral sofa, and two double beds. ❖ On our final night, we sat on our deck and watched early July Fourth fireworks exploding east and west. There will be other trips to far-flung places, but sometimes staying close to home, drinking wine beneath the stars as the baby monitor glows beside us, is adventure enough.

KATHLEEN BURGE, *Globe Staff*

Ocean View Inn & Resort

Getaway 28

171 Atlantic Road,
Gloucester, Mass.
978-283-6200 or 800-315-7557
www.oceanviewinnandresort.com

RATES
62 rooms. Varies seasonally, $95-280.

WHAT WE LIKED MOST
The view of lumbering waves swelling and crashing on the rocky shore.

WHAT WE LIKED LEAST
The lingering smell of disinfectant in the room.

WHAT SURPRISED US
How far away the city seemed.

YOU KNOW YOU'RE AT THE OCEAN VIEW INN & RESORT WHEN... seagulls wheel past, inches from your window.

THINGS TO REMEMBER
_____
_____
_____
_____
_____

MAINE • NEW HAMPSHIRE • VERMONT • **MASS**

AS WE WHEELED DOWN ATLANTIC ROAD, we spied a number of "For Sale" signs on green lawns across from the ocean. We could almost hear the agents chanting, "Location, location, location." Never was the mantra so true as on the winding road that traces the granite jaw of Cape Ann on Gloucester's "back side." Apart from the twin lighthouses on Thacher Island to the northeast, there's nothing between this coast and Europe except the ocean. That view must have been what attracted brothers John and Alexander Bowler, Worcester brewing magnates, to build their summer homes practically next door to each other across the road from a field of Brobdingnagian boulders trailing off into the crashing sea. Alexander's half-timbered Tudor-style "Twin Light Manor" functions as the main house of the Ocean View Inn and Resort complex. John's "High Cliff Lodge," which has five guest rooms always rented as a group, serves as the function hall.

❖ The public areas of Twin Light, which was completed in 1910, constitute a perfect Edwardian set piece with dark-stained woodwork, large fireplaces framed in brick or stone, a vast sitting room filled with Craftsman furniture, a clubby billiard room, rough stone walls in the dining room, and a scattering of small stained-glass windows. ❖ There was a tiny elevator, but we walked up to our big, third-floor front-corner room. When we opened the door, we barely noticed the room or its sloping ceiling under the gables. A large square window flanked by two small casement windows directed our eyes to the surf on the rocks below. ❖ The resort has immense curb appeal, and one feels transported to another time and place: a genuine getaway from 21st-century life in the city. Our room, while impeccably clean, needed updating. The beige brocade-pattern vinyl wallpaper blended with the green and beige brocade cover on the king-size bed, which blended with the pale finish on the French Provincial-style furniture. In short, the room was all about the view. ❖ The resort property has a swimming pool planted among its single-story motel units, but it's also a short drive to Good Harbor Beach for ocean swimming. ❖ The resort's Ocean's Edge Restaurant stretches across the front of the mansion and is all glassed-in for a matchless ocean view. When we came down in the morning for breakfast, we took a window seat and settled modestly for coffee, tea, and English muffins. With a single egg starting at $6.95, diners most definitely pay for their window onto the sea. But, then, the view is what it's all about.

PATRICIA HARRIS AND DAVID LYON, *Globe Correspondents*

Captain Jack's Wharf

Getaway 29

*73A Commercial St.,
Provincetown, Mass.
508-487-1450
www.provincetown.com/captjacks*

RATES
Open Memorial Day through Sept. 30. Seasonal weekly range, $700-$2,600; $100-$258 per night off-season.

WHAT WE LIKED MOST
The ramshackle charm, the sounds of the water, and the sense of history that permeates the place.

WHAT WE LIKED LEAST
The fact that the place fills up so quickly, and that we can rent only by the week in high season.

WHAT SURPRISED US
The overwhelming sense of peace and quiet, even with so many other cabins occupied.

YOU KNOW YOU'RE AT CAPTAIN JACK'S WHARF WHEN ... *the water flows right under your room, and there is deck space everywhere you look.*

THINGS TO REMEMBER

MAINE • NEW HAMPSHIRE • VERMONT • **MASS**

IF TENNESSEE WILLIAMS WERE STILL AROUND, he'd find Captain Jack's Wharf a changed place. The rambling little rooms stretched out over the water still have the same extraordinary view of the tidal flats and harbor that they did in the 1940s, when Williams camped here. But while the playwright wrote a friend about "an extraordinary all-night party" on the wharf, these days such a thing might get him thrown out on his ear. ❖ On the list of rules for guests of this charming vacation rental property in Provincetown's West End is this: "Please don't invite crowds of nonresident visitors to the Wharf." ❖ Understandable, really. Because what was built as storage for fishermen at the turn of the 19th century and later became a speakeasy known as the Circus Bar is now a dozen condominiums worth hundreds of thousands of dollars. Their owners surely want to protect their investment. Still, visitors can rent them by the week or, during the shoulder season, for a few days at a time. ❖ Be forewarned: Captain Jack's has so much character you might not feel the need to leave. A friend and I checked into a second-floor space dubbed Sunrise for a long weekend in mid-June and were instantly charmed. ❖ At Captain Jack's, on the water means on the water, which means heavenly sleeping amid sounds of the tide. Inside, Sunrise's open plan puts a double bed on one end near a tiny bathroom, a kitchen and dining area in the middle, and a little daybed and book-lined reading area leading to the deck on the other end. With paint-splattered floors and multicolored wooden chairs around the dining table, Sunrise seems like an artist's cottage, the kind of place you come to get inspiration and write a novel. ❖ The condos are called "cabins" for good reason, since they have neither air conditioning nor heat, and the bathroom, particularly, feels a little like camping. Still, we were able to throw a dinner party for a half-dozen friends who were in town. The kitchen comes equipped with all the basic necessities: pots, pans, glasses, plates, and silverware — and there's a little boom box (but no TV) for ambience. ❖ The food and conversation were a hit, but as the night wore on, the clock could be felt ticking; another of the posted rules states: "Wharf quiet hours are from 10 p.m. to 10 a.m." If we wanted the party going, it had to move elsewhere. But by that point we were ready, again, to hear nothing but the sound of water lapping the shore.

JOE YONAN, *Globe Staff*

Pentagoet Inn

Getaway 30

26 Main St.,
Castine, Maine
207-326-8616 or 800-845-1701
www.pentagoet.com

RATES
16 rooms. Open May to October; $115-$245.

WHAT WE LIKED MOST
An abundance of bicycles available for touring lovely Castine.

WHAT WE LIKED LEAST
The clattering of the cottage's screen door in the morning.

WHAT SURPRISED US
Owner Jack Burke's path from Maine to Asia and Africa and back again.

YOU KNOW YOU'RE AT PENTAGOET INN WHEN... Lenin keeps a watchful eye from his portrait on a wall of the inn's pub.

THINGS TO REMEMBER

MAINE • NEW HAMPSHIRE • VERMONT • MASS

LENIN WAS FOLLOWING US. As we moved from the bar to a table under a flat-bladed fan, the Russian revolutionary's eyes peered out from a portrait and seemed to track our steps. ❖ There were others: Queen Victoria, Gandhi, Sadat, Mobutu, Castro — a kaleidoscope, we would learn, of the barkeep's travels. Jack Burke, 53, a former relief worker in Asia and Africa, collected the portraits in bazaars and the occasional embassy. They now hang in the Passports Pub of the Pentagoet Inn, which he co-owns with his wife, Julie Van de Graaf. ❖ A whimsical Victorian in a town full of symmetrical Colonials and Georgians, the Pentagoet Inn has traditional trappings, but offers delightful twists. Foreign Affairs magazine is available for guests. And the bar, with its rattan furniture, lazy fans, and visages of foreign dignitaries, feels more like an expatriate hangout than a genteel inn on the Maine coast. ❖ The Pentagoet is one of the livelier spots after dark in Castine, a wonderfully uncluttered town perched on Penobscot Bay. We were glad to have gotten the last reservation for dinner on Saturday. The grilled scallops were jumbo-sized and flavorful, with a hint of anise; the slow-cooked lamb shank was tender. For dessert, we chose mango sorbet, so fresh tasting that we asked if it was made on-site. It was. ❖ We had chosen a room in the cottage behind the inn, the older of the Pentagoet's two buildings, built in 1791. The room was modest in size but felt spacious with three open windows drawing a breeze. The antique furnishings made the space feel neither spare nor overstuffed. ❖ Breakfast was a buffet of zucchini bread, bacon, eggs, granola with fruit and yogurt, and freshly squeezed orange juice. Afterward we found Burke behind the bar, and he related his story: Raised in Portland, he read a National Geographic story about oil rigging, and after graduating high school, headed to Houston to become a roughneck. Oil rigging took him around the globe, including Thailand, where he began working with refugees. Under the aegis of United Nations agencies, Burke traveled throughout Asia and Africa and collected mementos. He gave up refugee work after the embassy bombings in Kenya and Tanzania in 1998, and in 2000 they bought the inn. He still travels extensively in winter, when the inn is closed. ❖ We thought of Burke as we drove out of Castine, past the Maine Maritime Academy that sends young men and women to far-flung points. It seemed fitting that Burke had hung his memories in the town, giving guests at the Pentagoet something to wonder and dream about.

SARAH SCHWEITZER, *Globe Staff*

The Richards

Getaway 31

144 Gibson Ave.,
Narragansett, R.I.
401-789-7746
www.therichardsbnb.com

RATES
Four rooms. Doubles $130-$170,
two-bedroom suite $230.

WHAT WE LIKED MOST
The feeling of being in an English country manor right out of "Wuthering Heights."

WHAT WE LIKED LEAST
Not being able to lock the bedroom door.

WHAT SURPRISED US
The extensive gardens and landscaping.

YOU KNOW YOU'RE AT THE RICHARDS WHEN... *you half expect to hear someone shouting "Heathcliff!" across the moors.*

THINGS TO REMEMBER

THE VISION CAME TO HIM IN A DREAM. And it was so powerful that Joseph Peace Hazard had no choice but to build the stone mansion, not for his own residence but as a place where someone else might find shelter, a place he would name "Druidsdream." The striking home, dating from 1884 and built from stone quarried on the property, is on the National Register of Historic Places and today operates as a bed-and-breakfast, The Richards, run by Steven and Nancy Richards. ❖ Everything in this 8,500-square-foot house is big: The ceilings are high, the hallways are spacious, and the banisters are wide. Common rooms include a stunning dining room overlooking the gardens and filled with Nancy Richards's auction finds. Her collection of dragons adds a whimsical touch. ❖ Our second-floor room had a four-poster queen bed with a crocheted canopy and a daybed, made up with sheets at our request. Plaids and big floral prints in salmon and yellow contrasted nicely with the soft lemon walls. All the rooms have fireplaces, but regulations prohibit their use, Richards said. ❖ Our large, private, L-shaped bath with a shower was down the hall. The cabinet contained an unusual mishmash of toiletries. Next to the bathroom was a guest refrigerator, and just outside our room was a rack of brochures on area attractions. We were surprised by the absence of a television in the house. ❖ We're all for neighborliness, but it bothered us that there was no lock on the bedroom door, nor was there any way to indicate if we did not want to be disturbed. ❖ Breakfast is served family-style at precisely 8:45 a.m. We enjoyed coffee and juice, fresh strawberries, muffins, pancakes, and bacon one morning, and an egg-and-cheese strata the next. ❖ For dinner, Richards recommended the Coast Guard House, a Narragansett institution on the ocean. The specialty is seafood, but there's a good selection of steaks as well. ❖ One of the pleasures of a stay at The Richards is meandering the gardens on the 1 1/2-acre property. There's a white garden, a water garden with koi, and a lovely shade garden. A half-mile path through the woods and across Ocean Road leads to a rocky ocean view. Beachcombers can walk, bicycle, or drive to Narragansett Town Beach, less than a mile away, though it's pricey at $5 per person plus $6 to park. Richards also sends guests to Scarborough Beach, a little less expensive and just as lovely.

ELLEN ALBANESE, *Globe Staff*

Grey Havens Inn

Getaway 32

Seguinland Road,
Georgetown, Maine
207-371-2616 or 800-431-2316
www.greyhavens.com

RATES
14 guestrooms. Open May to early November; $160-$280 per night, two-night minimum on weekends.

WHAT WE LIKED MOST
The relaxed hospitality of the innkeepers.

WHAT WE LIKED LEAST
We would have liked a fan to help cool our room at night.

WHAT SURPRISED US
The little glider for two below the slope of the lawn for great views and privacy.

YOU KNOW YOU'RE AT GREY HAVENS INN WHEN ... the innkeepers' 2-pound terrier, Wickett, skitters past on the front porch, getting her afternoon exercise.

THINGS TO REMEMBER

MAINE · NEW HAMPSHIRE · VERMONT · MASS

A GARLAND OF ROSES twined around the staircase banister and big bouquets sat on practically every table when we arrived at Grey Havens Inn on a Sunday afternoon. ❖ "There was a wedding here yesterday," Tiffany Dumas explained, "and we left the roses so our guests could enjoy them." Dumas, who is also a wedding photographer, grabbed one of our suitcases and called for her husband, Chris, to take the other. They bounded up the stairs to Room 14 on the third floor. ❖ In just their second year as resident innkeepers of Grey Havens, the Dumases' fresh enthusiasm for the hospitality trade still showed. Tiffany's parents purchased the landmark inn on a rocky bluff overlooking Sheepscot Bay in 2005. ❖ Built in 1904, Grey Havens is among the few shingle-style hotels still operating in New England, a distinction that earned it a spot on the National Register of Historic Places. But it's not so much the architecture as the relaxed seaside atmosphere that makes Grey Havens a timeless retreat. ❖ The cottage-style walls of our room glowed with the venerable gold of clear-varnished spruce beadboard. The same paneling on the ceiling was painted a light blue to mirror the blue of the bay, visible through a single window with lace curtains fluttering in the breeze. In the bathroom, the beadboard was painted white and the floors were covered in yellow-and-white-checkerboard linoleum squares. There was a shower stall, but no tub. On the wall-mounted sink, a large seashell served as a soap dish. ❖ Like most guests, we didn't spend many daylight hours in our room. The vast lounge has a floor-to-ceiling fireplace of smooth beach boulders at one end and a 12-foot window at the other to let in the view. That view is even better when accompanied by salty breezes on the broad wraparound porch, where we quickly laid claim to a couple of white wooden rockers. ❖ Nearby, a mother and daughter from Alabama consulted guidebooks to plan the next day. They might paddle a kayak up the sheltered fiord of Robinhood Cove, or jaunt up to the Maine Maritime Museum in Bath, or enjoy top-rated sand beaches at Reid State Park. ❖ Gigantic blueberry muffins graced the breakfast buffet table the next morning in the dining room, where the tables are covered in blue and white checked cloths. A baked egg dish, fruit bowl, cereals, pastries, and breads rounded out the spread. ❖ Mid-morning, when we said our goodbyes, the Alabamans were rocking away on the porch, still debating their options for the day. We bet they never budged. Why would they?

PATRICIA HARRIS AND DAVID LYON, *Globe Correspondents*

Newcastle Inn

Getaway 33

60 River Road,
Newcastle, Maine
207-563-5685 or 800-832-8669
www.newcastleinn.com

RATES
15 rooms and suites. Varies seasonally. $125–$255.

WHAT WE LIKED MOST
The elegant cheese plate at the inn restaurant.

WHAT WE LIKED LEAST
Some misleading advertising about the place.

WHAT SURPRISED US
The terrific cuisine and the many interesting trails in the area.

YOU KNOW YOU'RE AT THE NEWCASTLE INN WHEN . . . *the wallpaper talks back at you.*

THINGS TO REMEMBER
_____
_____
_____
_____

MAINE • **NEW HAMPSHIRE** • **VERMONT** • **MASS**

DURING OUR FIRST FEW HOURS at the Newcastle Inn, we thought we might have made a mistake. Our room, advertised as overlooking the Damariscotta River, mainly overlooked a parking lot with the river in the leafy distance. The inn itself, touted as a "historic 1860s' sea captain's home," had vinyl siding, gas fireplaces, and air conditioners sticking out of several windows. Its decor was lively and eclectic but hardly restful or conventionally historic. ❖ But gradually we began to warm to the place. For one thing, we ate dinner. Lupine's, the inn's little restaurant, was worth the trip to mid-coast Maine. ❖ Unlike many fine restaurant chefs who oversee operations but don't do much cooking themselves, Josh DeGroot puts his personal touch on everything that comes out of Lupine's kitchen. He makes excellent sorbets and ice creams, bakes his own breads, and shops daily at nearby farms and markets. ❖ The convenience and luxury of being able to crawl into bed after this meal, instead of making the long drive home, was sufficient reason to stay at the Newcastle Inn. It is owned and run by Laura and Peter Barclay, landscape designers who bought it three years ago. Laura always liked to entertain, and her husband says he decided she might as well get paid for it. They groomed the property, redecorated the interiors, hired DeGroot, and got other Barclay family members into the act. Breakfast, included in the room rate, was large and satisfying, with juice, a fruit course, a breakfast bread, coffee or tea, and an entrée: a choice of homemade granola or pancakes with sausage on our visit. ❖ The inn has 15 guest rooms, all with private baths, many with gas fireplaces, and two with Jacuzzis. All the rooms are individually decorated with lots of bold red, gold, green, and blue patterns. One room, the Monhegan Island, won an interior design award for its eclectic combination of colors, patterns, and textures. Our room was scantily equipped, no phones or TVs or the like, just a clock radio and a hair dryer. But lots of games were available in one of several pleasant common rooms. ❖ The inn has a lounge that opens onto a picturesque deck with tables and a nice river view. In warm weather, it would be a lovely spot for breakfast or appetizers before dinner. ❖ We were pleased to discover several interesting hiking trails a mile or two away. Our favorite was the Salt Bay Heritage Trail.

JUDITH GAINES, *Globe Correspondent*

Cliff Lodge

Getaway 34

9 Cliff Road,
Nantucket, Mass.
508-228-9480
www.clifflodgenantucket.com

RATES
12 guestrooms. Varies seasonally, $95-$295.

WHAT WE LIKED MOST
The views from the top-floor room and from the spectacular widow's walk.

WHAT WE LIKED LEAST
The tiny room, although bigger ones are available for those with foresight.

WHAT SURPRISED US
The peacefulness of the patio and the affordability of the place, even in high season.

YOU KNOW YOU'RE AT THE CLIFF LODGE WHEN . . . you can see Nantucket Sound from the rooftop.

THINGS TO REMEMBER
___
___
___
___
___

A 10-MINUTE WALK FROM THE FERRIES on Straight Wharf takes you through the little downtown, past the guys hawking bike rentals, past a landscape gardener at work on a home's curb appeal, and then up a hill, where the Cliff Lodge is all verticality. ❖ A curving staircase leads to the tiny front porch and then into the little entryway. The place opens up a little in the sunny sitting room and dining room, but it's not until you climb up a couple of flights of stairs and onto the widow's walk that the significance of the inn's spyglass logo comes into focus, so to speak. The astonishing view extends beyond the town and harbor all the way to Nantucket Sound. ❖ It's a fitting amenity for an inn built as a sea captain's house in 1771. Back then, according to the Cliff Lodge's promotional materials, the family who lived there could witness such historic moments as the landing of the redcoats in Nantucket Harbor. Unfortunately, I'm visiting during the Nantucket Film Festival, and the movie crowd means that I didn't have my pick of the rooms. Mine is nestled in what seems like the rafters. Everything is built in. It's an efficient use of space, and the best part is the view: Through the single window I can see dozens of rooftops and even the water. ❖ Breakfast is a self-serve affair. The granola is full of dried fruit and nuts, the coffee is good and strong, and there's juice, bread, and jam. It's enough to fortify me as I trek to Jetties Beach, Brant Point Light, and then back into town for more coffee. I return to take a nap, then poke into some of the other rooms, which are bright, cheery, and all more comfortable-looking than mine. Note to self: Next time, plan. ❖ The common areas of the inn have some nifty nooks, such as a sunroom off one hallway and two big leather chairs and a bookcase off the main stairs. In the entryway, a crystal platter holds some delectable cookies. And outside, four tables sit on a peaceful red-brick patio, ringed with flowering bushes. ❖ There's so much birdsong and leaf-rustling out here that I find myself almost nodding off to sleep, until a flash of color catches my eye. A robin lights on one of the tables near me, looks around, and flies away. I'm not sure where he's off to, but if I were him, I'd wing it up to that widow's walk, where everything in sight looks perfect.

JOE YONAN, *Globe Staff*

Beach Rose Inn

Getaway 35

17 Chase Road,
West Falmouth, Mass.
508-540-5706 or 800-498-5706
www.thebeachroseinn.com

RATES
Eight rooms and one cottage. Open early April to mid-December, $140-$250.

WHAT WE LIKED MOST
The quiet residential location close to beaches and Falmouth village.

WHAT WE LIKED LEAST
The feeling that we were intruding on the innkeepers' quarters when we turned on the television in the guest den.

WHAT SURPRISED US
Learning that the inn was about to be sold.

YOU KNOW YOU'RE AT THE BEACH ROSE INN WHEN . . . *a breezy porch with a blue ceiling makes you feel as if you are outdoors.*

THINGS TO REMEMBER

SOMETIMES THE SECRECY BACKFIRES. For this column, Globe writers visit inns anonymously to make sure they experience the accommodations as readers would. At the end of their stays, they can reveal their identities and the purpose of the visit. ❖ When I told innkeeper Donna McIlrath, after a Sunday morning breakfast of crepe-wrapped scrambled eggs, that we were planning to run a review of the Beach Rose Inn, she was surprised and crestfallen. "We're selling the inn!" she wailed. ❖ The new owners, Douglas and Sheryll Reichwein, have preserved most aspects of the inn and added features designed to make this pleasant hideaway even more enjoyable. ❖ Tucked away on a side street off Route 28A, the inn offers the peace and quiet of a residential neighborhood just five minutes from the beach and 10 minutes from the town center. The 1863 farmhouse, listed on the National Register of Historic Places, is white with deep pink shutters and trim and bordered by a white picket fence. A path of crushed shells leads to the front door. ❖ One of the inn's charming features is an enclosed bow porch with a robin's egg-blue ceiling and wicker furniture. Breakfast is served here and in the attached breakfast room with its lace-curtained windows and an old-fashioned stove in the corner. Guests have use of a parlor and a tiny TV room.
❖ There are four guest rooms in the main house, four in the carriage house, and a housekeeping cottage that rents by the week, as well as an unheated apartment. ❖ We stayed in the Quisset Room, which had a queen-size bed, nightstand, dresser, upholstered chair, and reading light crammed into a 9-by-12-foot space. The bathroom, on the other hand, was huge. ❖ Decor was simple but thoughtful. There was an old-fashioned brush, comb, and mirror set atop a crocheted runner on the dresser and lots of accent pieces on the white walls, such as dried flowers in frames, a miniature bonnet, and a eucalyptus wreath over the headboard.
❖ The inn's top accommodation is the Highland Room in the carriage house, with a queen canopy bed, whirlpool for two, electric fireplace, and small refrigerator. But we were smitten with the Falmouth Suite, with its blue-and-white linens and private porch. ❖ At the innkeepers' recommendation, we had dinner at the Chapoquoit Grill just down the road. This hip, busy, friendly place offers seafood, brick-oven pizza, and interesting twists on American bistro fare. Entrees run $9.50 to $25.

ELLEN ALBANESE, *Globe Staff*

Warfield House Inn
at Valley View Farm

Getaway 36

200 Warfield Road,
Charlemont, Mass.
413-339-6600 or 888-339-8439
www.warfieldhouseinn.com

RATES
Seven rooms in the main house, $99–$125; two rooms in the nearby bungalow, $99–$150.

WHAT WE LIKED MOST
With extremely limited cellphone service, the farm seems at just the right remove from the 21st century.

WHAT WE LIKED LEAST
Little space for toiletries in the bathroom.

WHAT SURPRISED US
Exotic animals such as emus and llamas among the chickens, sheep, and cattle.

YOU KNOW YOU'RE AT WARFIELD HOUSE INN WHEN... the innkeeper invites young guests to help her collect eggs in the henhouse early in the morning.

THINGS TO REMEMBER

MAINE · NEW HAMPSHIRE · VERMONT · MASS

THE SWEET SCENT OF TIMOTHY AND CLOVER hung in the air when we arrived at the Warfield House Inn at the end of a steep road off the Mohawk Trail. "This is still a working farm," innkeeper Dottie Footit told us. "They've just finished the second haying of the season." ❖ Edward Warfield picked this broad hillside as his farm site in 1869 and great-grandson John Warfield Glaze has kept the farm in operation while adding a restaurant and wedding pavilion. Glaze has continued taking in boarders, a tradition that began in the 1930s when a bigger house replaced the original farmhouse destroyed in a fire. ❖ Our room, No. 7, was one of two new rooms up steep, narrow stairs on the farmhouse's third floor. Tucked under the eaves, it merged the charm and character of sloping walls and a pitched ceiling with modern amenities such as remote-controlled air-conditioning and a ceiling fan. The large room featured a snug sitting area in an alcove with a pair of windows looking westward to the Berkshire Hills. ❖ The farm's main focus is beef cattle, but Herefords were grazing in a distant pasture. In the gentleman farmer tradition, Glaze keeps a menagerie of unusual breeds. Footit pointed out a shaggy Highland cow before we reached a paddock where two Haflinger horses whinnied for hay. "A lot of brides like to ride in a carriage pulled by the horses," Footit said. ❖ We returned to the farmhouse and strolled downhill to the big red building that holds the Hawk's Nest Pub and the casual Charlemont Room restaurant. Antique farm implements on the walls accentuate the country setting. Meals start with a fluffy buttermilk biscuit and some of the farm's own maple syrup. ❖ The menu ranges from sandwiches, pizzas, and pastas to such entrees as chicken marsala and filet mignon, but the bargain-priced country dinners best fit the setting. One of us chose ground sirloin and the other Southern fried chicken breast. Both homey plates featured mashed potatoes with gravy, and broccoli as the vegetable of the day. The chicken was perfectly crunchy on the outside, delectably moist on the interior. The beef, which comes from the farm's herd, was lean and intensely flavored. ❖ The next morning, Footit served us scrambled eggs, English muffins, and sausage in the dining room of the farmhouse. "These are our own eggs," she said. "But we've run out of our own sausage." We were reminded of a comment she'd made on our farm tour: "This is a working farm. I never get too attached to the animals."

PATRICIA HARRIS AND DAVID LYON, *Globe Correspondents*

The Lauren

Getaway 37

3 Church St.,
Woodstock, Vt.
802-457-1925
www.thelaureninn.com

RATES
10 rooms. Varies seasonally, $169-$375.

WHAT WE LIKED MOST
The rooms were spacious and stylish with modern amenities, while retaining a simple New England charm.

WHAT WE LIKED LEAST
The service, though well-meaning, was haphazard at best and absent at worst.

WHAT SURPRISED US
The excellent cuisine.

YOU KNOW YOU'RE AT THE LAUREN WHEN... *you sit on the back porch and view a wide sweep of lawn leading down to the pool and the Ottauquechee River.*

THINGS TO REMEMBER

MAINE • NEW HAMPSHIRE • **VERMONT** • MASS

THE LAUREN WILL PROBABLY BE a great place to stay someday. We feel confident in that statement, even though our visit to the inn when it was still in its infancy suffered from several inconveniences that appeared to be start-up related. ❖ Our room, No. 5, was large and lovely, with a high ceiling, five windows, couch, and wonderfully comfortable king-size bed. Sage green walls, wide white window casings, white linens, and black contemporary furniture gave the place a sophisticated look and a relaxed feel. A flat screen TV with DVD player and radio with iPod station worked fine. ❖ The bathroom had white tiles and polished metal fixtures, and was impeccably clean, though we needed extra towels before heading into town for dinner. We went downstairs and rang the bell. We rang again. It was eerily quiet at 8 p.m. We ended up sharing a towel until we found someone to ask in the morning. ❖ That person was Peter Shoemaker, the cheerful manager, breakfast server, and chief bottle-washer. The inn's owner is Jack Maiden, who with his wife, Nicole, also owns the Kedron Valley Inn in South Woodstock. (Shoemaker shuttles between properties.) We learned that someone would fix the balky phone in our room that morning and someone else would repair the pool that afternoon. (Earlier, we had strolled across the lush lawn to where the pool is beautifully set along the Ottauquechee River adjacent to the tennis court, only to find the water dirty.) ❖ Breakfast is included and is served in the elegantly appointed dining room. Choice of an omelet, eggs, or pancakes was offered along with juice and excellent organic coffee.❖ The inn is trying to establish itself as a culinary destination, and judging from one meal, it has done an excellent job. The spinach gnocchi were delicate pouches piled atop an intensely flavorful basil cream and pancetta sauce. Beets with blue cheese emulsion were five tangy, sweet, button-sized bites that looked like small ice cream sandwiches. But we really swooned over the hanger steak with roasted garlic, mainly because thin slices of the local Green Mountain Blue Cheese were the perfect accompaniment. ❖ Also in the plus column, the inn is located near the green in the center of town, only blocks from the shopping district. ❖ Before leaving, Connie Maiden, mother of the owner, gave us a tour of the other rooms, each stylishly designed by her son. Would we go back? You bet. Minus a few kinks, the place is bound to be splendid.

NECEE REGIS, *Globe Correspondent*

Bass Cottage Inn

Getaway 38

14 The Field,
Bar Harbor, Maine
866-782-9224 or 207-288-1234
www.basscottage.com

RATES
10 rooms. Varies seasonally, $175-$350.

WHAT WE LIKED MOST
The sprawling elegance of the first-floor living rooms tied for best with the breakfast muffins.

WHAT WE LIKED LEAST
The central air conditioning can't be turned off in the bedrooms.

WHAT SURPRISED US
How quiet and peaceful it is, only steps away from Main Street in busy Bar Harbor.

YOU KNOW YOU'RE AT THE BASS COTTAGE INN WHEN... *owner Jeff Anderholm welcomes you with his mile-wide smile.*

THINGS TO REMEMBER

MAINE • NEW HAMPSHIRE • VERMONT • MASS

WHEN I FIRST MET JEFF ANDERHOLM he was wearing a Hawaiian shirt and a big smile and I was immediately suspicious. Before I even had pulled my bags out of the car he whisked me into the spacious parlor of the Bass Cottage Inn to show me the luscious woodwork, the high ceilings, the fireplace, and the light-filled dining room where breakfast is served. ❖ Had he recognized my name when I registered? Did he know I was there to review his inn? Why else would he be so welcoming? It turns out my suspicions were misguided; the man simply loves his job. ❖ The inn, I learned in my first three minutes, was built as a private home in 1885, and subsequently operated as an inn owned by one local family from 1928 until 2003. That's when Anderholm and his wife, Teri, purchased the building and, putting aside their lives as business executives in Boston, began a meticulous, yearlong renovation. ❖ The tour continued past the check-in desk to another room with a fireplace, leather chairs, an oriental carpet, and a stained glass panel in the ceiling. Through this room is a pantry, stocked with dark-roasted coffee, tea, and a mini-fridge filled with water, soft drinks, and a pitcher of brewed ice tea. ❖ My room featured a television (a free DVD library was downstairs), phone (free local calls), bathroom (a shower — no tub, an abundance of towels, and a robe), and a queen-size bed beneath a vaulted ceiling. My room, No. 7 on the third floor, is one of the inn's smallest, but was plenty big for me. The decorating scheme is soothing and low-key, in pale pink, beige, and white. The decorative bed pillows, bedspread, and window treatments have subtle floral patterns but aren't frilly. ❖ Breakfast is served from 8 to 9:30 a.m. Muffins, fruit, and juice accompanied the hot entree choices one egg item and one waffle item each morning, both beautifully presented. ❖ The inn is steps away from Bar Harbor's busy Main Street and it's also steps from the harbor, where whale-watching boats, kayakers, and ferries arrive and depart. ❖ On the morning of my departure I revealed to Anderholm the hidden purpose of my visit. ❖ "I saw you taking notes at breakfast a few minutes ago, and the thought crossed my mind that you might be a travel writer," he said. "Then I looked at you and decided: 'Nah.' " Which proves that looks can be deceiving, but at the Bass Cottage Inn what you see is what you get, which is pretty darn wonderful.

NECEE REGIS, *Globe Correspondent*

Red Maple Inn

Getaway 39

217 Main St.,
Spencer, Mass.
508-885-9205
www.theredmapleinn.com

RATES
Six rooms. $119-$249.

WHAT WE LIKED MOST
The warmth and hospitality of the innkeepers.

WHAT WE LIKED LEAST
Wrestling with the cord of the hair dryer on a wall in the bathroom.

WHAT SURPRISED US
Hearing jazz and blues from the 1940s, a refreshing change from the classical music most bed-and-breakfasts favor.

YOU KNOW YOU'RE AT THE RED MAPLE INN WHEN... each time you enter a room you're dazzled anew by the charmingly over-the-top decor.

THINGS TO REMEMBER

COUNTING THE TWO IN THE BATHROOM, there were eight mirrors in our room at the Red Maple Inn. And a gilded Japanese screen of cranes and cherry blossoms, next to an exotic arrangement of dried plants in burgundy and gold. And four tall, slim lamps with tasseled shades. Even the bed skirt was fringed with beads. ❖ In true Victorian fashion, no surface is left undecorated in this Colonial mansion listed on the National Register of Historic Places. It is replete with intense colors and rich fabrics. John Bills, who owns the inn with his wife, Shari Alexander, said the couple's goal was to make sure that anyone sitting in any of the inn's rooms would have "something pretty to look at." They have succeeded to the point where a weekend is barely enough time to take in all the baubles and beads, glitter and glass. ❖ We stayed in the Duck Room, which featured bisque ducks in flight on teal green wallpaper, a duck print border, brass fireplace tools fashioned with duck heads, and a duck-shaped tissue box holder. It became a bit of a game for my husband and me to find all the duck accents in the room. ❖ The queen sleigh bed had wrought iron scrollwork in the headboard and footboard. There was a big closet, with robes, and a dresser with a small television and DVD player. The inn has more than 700 movies on DVD that guests can borrow. An antique sewing machine served as a bedside table. We sensed that someone had fun putting this room together. ❖ Each evening we selected the next day's breakfast from a menu hung on our door. Choices included omelet Florentine, smoked ham and cheese scramble, raisin bread French toast, and homemade granola, along with sausage, croissants, and muffins. ❖ Long before she was an innkeeper, Alexander was a chef, and she offers custom dinners by advance reservation. The week before our visit we received a menu asking us to choose appetizers and entrees. Tenderloin of beef was rich and moist, sauced with a cabernet demi-glace and accompanied by roasted potato pancakes. Jumbo shrimp stuffed with Spanish Manchego cheese and wrapped in prosciutto was a recipe Alexander picked up in Spain. ❖ It's obvious that Bills and Alexander love what they do. He had a warm smile and helpful information each time we met, and she delighted in recounting the stories behind the dishes she served. For guests, that passion can turn a pleasant visit into a memorable one.

ELLEN ALBANESE, *Globe Staff*

Inn at Danbury

Getaway 40

67 Route 104,
Danbury, N.H.
603-768-3318 or 866-326-2879
www.innatdanbury.com

RATES
13 rooms. $95-$160.

WHAT WE LIKED MOST
The true country tavern feel of the dining room.

WHAT WE LIKED LEAST
The surprising level of road noise from Route 104.

WHAT SURPRISED US
The large dimensions of the indoor pool.

YOU KNOW YOU'RE AT THE INN AT DANBURY WHEN... the aroma of fresh-baked bread makes you forget entirely about dieting.

THINGS TO REMEMBER
_____
_____
_____
_____
_____

THE INNKEEPERS CALL ROOM NO. 10 in the Inn at Danbury the "love nest," thanks in no small part to the king-size bed and freestanding gas fireplace. ❖ Sure enough, as we perused the comments book left on a low dresser, it became clear that many previous guests had gravitated to this room for a honeymoon, romantic escape, or anniversary getaway. ❖ One couple, marking 35 years (and four children) together, even passed along a cryptic hint for marital longevity. "Husbands: Can I give you some advice?" they wrote. "Pay attention! That's it, that's the advice: Pay attention!" ❖ We had only to look to innkeepers Bob and Alexandra Graf for a model of hard-working harmony. He's a former ski instructor and general contractor and she is a Dutch-born former flight attendant and Mrs. Salt Lake City. With their four kids in tow, they left Utah to take over the inn in 2002. What makes the inn feel most homey are the aromas wafting from the kitchen, where Bob makes breakfast and soon thereafter launches into baking bread for the evening diners in the inn's restaurant. ❖ In the Alphorn Bistro, Bob Graf draws on his grandmother's recipes for German comfort food. The menu offers many variations on sausages and schnitzels, sauerkraut, sweet red cabbage, boiled potatoes, and spatzle. We opted for sauerbraten (only offered as a special because it takes five days to marinate the beef) and a mixed plate of wurst and schnitzel. ❖ The hearty dishes proved absolutely authentic, right down to the mild spicing. We guessed that desserts would be luscious, and neither the apple strudel nor the chocolate Bavarian cream disappointed. ❖ The Grafs encourage guests to take dessert back to their rooms, so we climbed a flight of stairs to the "love nest." Located at the front of the inn, the simply furnished, L-shaped room has a step-out balcony, a low dresser and a highboy, two comfortable wing-back chairs flanking the fireplace, and small tables beside the iron-frame king-size bed. ❖ We knew it was time for breakfast when the aroma of bacon wafted up the stairs. Bob was at the stove again, ready to prepare pancakes or eggs any way we wanted them as Alex chatted with the guests. She expressed excitement at visiting the Eastern States Expo in Springfield, Mass., to give a cooking demonstration. ❖ "Sometimes," she said, "it is good to get away, just the two of you." ❖ Bob stood in the doorway with plates of pancakes. And he was paying attention.

PATRICIA HARRIS AND DAVID LYON, *Globe Correspondents*

Inn at Crystal Lake

Getaway 41

*2356 Eaton Road,
Eaton, N.H.
603-447-2120 or 800-343-7336
www.innatcrystallake.com*

RATES
11 rooms. Varies seasonally, $109-$239.

WHAT WE LIKED MOST
The inn restaurant's excellent food and cozy attached pub.

WHAT WE LIKED LEAST
Our cramped, narrow bathroom.

WHAT SURPRISED US
The homemade cookies in our room when we arrived.

YOU KNOW YOU'RE AT INN AT CRYSTAL LAKE WHEN... *you spot the lake, a lovely place for swimming and canoeing, across from the inn.*

THINGS TO REMEMBER
_____
_____
_____
_____

MAINE · **NEW HAMPSHIRE** · VERMONT · MASS

I KNEW I WAS GOING TO LIKE THIS PLACE as soon as we arrived late on a Friday night, ragged after a rainy two-hour drive from Boston, and found a plate of homemade oatmeal-raisin cookies in our room. ❖ There wasn't a crumb left by morning. ❖ The cookies were the handiwork of Bobby Barker, who's also behind the Inn at Crystal Lake's sensational sugar-dusted blueberry muffins, custardy cheddar quiche, and pancakes so naturally sweet they're delicious even without maple syrup. Barker owns this White Mountains inn with his partner, Tim Ostendorf, who doubles as bartender and breakfast server, among other roles. ❖ One June weekend, we were enticed by the inn's "wildlife and bird-watching mud season special," a two-night, $295 package. The price included the room, two breakfasts, one dinner, one lunch, and an adorable gift bag of Audubon Society trail maps, a guide to wildlife refuges, insect-repelling body lotion, lavender goat milk soap, and, in a cute final touch, birdseed. If the goal was to charm us, mission accomplished. ❖ The package's outdoorsy theme was the perfect opportunity for our first White Mountains hike of the year. The inn is a 45-minute drive from Pinkham Notch, a trailhead for several great climbs, and five miles from bustling North Conway, home to hordes of gift shops, restaurants, hotels, and outlet stores. ❖ Barker and Ostendorf bought the inn — a handsome, four-story, yellow-clapboard house built in 1884 — five years ago, and opened an on-site restaurant in 2003. Townspeople often stop by to dine, making the inn a central part of the tiny town of Eaton, which consists of little more than a church, a cemetery, and a general store. It's an excellent restaurant with a real chef, lovely dining room, and snug bar, the Palmer House Pub, packed with eye-grabbing knickknacks. In previous lives, the inn was variously a private home, a library, a post office, and a boarding school; our third-floor bedroom, in fact, was once part of a boys' dormitory. Comfortable and carpeted, it had a double bed, bureau, rocking chair, side table, TV, and VCR. We especially liked the modern window air conditioner that we could set to a precise temperature. ❖ The Inn at Crystal Lake isn't a destination for luxury pampering; it's a place of simple comforts, no-pressure hospitality, easy access to some of the state's most beautiful outdoor spots, and great cooking. It also offers plenty of thoughtful amenities, like beach towels and beach chairs for guests to use at Crystal Lake, right across the street.

SACHA PFEIFFER, *Globe Staff*

Encore Bed & Breakfast

Getaway 42

116 West Newton St.,
Boston, Mass.
617-247-3425
www.encorebandb.com

RATES
Prices range from $140 to $210, depending on season and length of stay.

WHAT WE LIKED MOST
The Bang & Olufsen radio with remote control that we worked from the bed.

WHAT WE LIKED LEAST
Having to choose the night before what time we wanted breakfast.

WHAT SURPRISED US
How easy it was to feel like we were on vacation in our hometown.

YOU KNOW YOU'RE AT ENCORE BED & BREAKFAST WHEN . . . your room is named after a famous composer, playwright, or choreographer.

THINGS TO REMEMBER
_____
_____
_____
_____

SOMETIMES YOU WANT TO GET AWAY in your own hometown. It's amazing how a mere mile and a half change of perspective can enhance your appreciation of the city. ❖ That's how we arrived at Encore Bed & Breakfast in Boston's South End, a neighborhood we previously enjoyed only as a place to go out for dinner, or as a somewhat confusing series of streets to navigate while traveling from point A to point B. ❖ The South End is the largest district of Victorian row houses on the National Register of Historic Places. Encore is in one of these 19th-century brick homes at one end of a quiet street between Tremont Street and Columbus Avenue. ❖ Encore has four rooms, each named after a 20th-century composer, playwright, or choreographer. Our room, the Bernstein, was on the third floor. A long, narrow room with exposed brick and hunter green and pale yellow walls, it felt spacious because three west-facing windows provided bright afternoon light. ❖ The room's furnishings were enough to make a modernist giddy: a pair of Marcel Breuer Wassily chairs flanked an Eileen Gray table made of glass and chrome tubular steel. In the common area, we found pale gray Philippe Starck Dr. No armchairs. ❖ If you think all this modernity feels cold, be assured that it doesn't. In the breakfast nook, the clean lines are tempered by a Moroccan rug and decorative masks collected by the owners. ❖ In the bedroom, wide-wood slat blinds, off-white cotton window treatments, and a decorative wool rug in green, yellow, and gray create a warm tone. In addition, colorful framed posters of theater and dance performances adorn each room. ❖ Encore's owners, Reinhold Mahler and David Miller, developed the space five years ago. Mahler, a retired architect and professor, greets you at the door and serves breakfast with his charming German accent (he emigrated in 1989). Miller has a day job with an investment company and at night runs a company in the Black Box theater at the nearby Boston Center for the Arts. ❖ A simple European-style breakfast is served each morning between 8 and 10. Each room is provided with a menu and choices to check off and leave on the counter the night before. ❖ Encore's location can't be beat. It's within easy walking distance of all the South End's great restaurants, shops, the BCA, and the Mills Gallery. There are many restaurants we'd like to try, which means the next time we stay at Encore, we'll have to book a room for an entire week. Can't wait.

NECEE REGIS, *Globe Correspondent*

Bow Street Inn

Getaway 43

121 Bow St.,
Portsmouth, N.H.
603-431-7760
www.bowstreetinn.com

RATES
10 rooms. Varies seasonally, $145-$180.

WHAT WE LIKED MOST
The central location, a short walk to shops, restaurants, and the waterfront.

WHAT WE LIKED LEAST
Having to move our car out of the church parking lot by 7:30 a.m. Sunday.

WHAT SURPRISED US
How quiet it was in our room despite the fact that the inn sits above a theater.

YOU KNOW YOU'RE AT THE BOW STREET INN WHEN... you can catch a play without leaving the property.

THINGS TO REMEMBER
_____
_____
_____
_____
_____

MAINE • NEW HAMPSHIRE • VERMONT • MASS

YOU DON'T HAVE TO KNOW MUCH about real estate to know the best things about the Bow Street Inn are location, location, and location. ❖ The inn sits above the Seacoast Repertory Theatre in a 19th-century brick building in the city's historic district (inn guests receive discounted tickets to shows). It's so close to the shore you can smell the Piscataqua River. A few minutes' walk along narrow brick streets takes you to Strawbery Banke, downtown restaurants, and the docks. And you can leave your car in a church parking lot across the street — at least until 7:30 Sunday morning. ❖ The inn's approach is simple but practical, even thoughtful. Directions were easy to follow. Newspaper clippings about new or unusual attractions and restaurants were posted on a bulletin board in the lobby. Joan and Arthur Jones bought the inn in 1998, after they retired from jobs in nursing and teaching in Buffalo and "fell in love with Portsmouth," Joan Jones said. ❖ Our room was plain but comfortable. It had a queen-size bed and a small loveseat, along with a butcher block table and chair. A shelf unit held a chest of drawers, small television, and compact refrigerator. The mattress was firm and the lamps on the night tables provided good reading light. There was a phone, and local calls were free. ❖ The bathroom was small but adequate, with a tub and shower. Toiletries included inn-brand soap and conditioning shampoo. Nice thick towels and a hair dryer completed the amenities. Lighting over the sink, however, was so dim as to make it virtually impossible to apply makeup.

The inn's premier accommodation is Room 7, a suite with a partial water view, which is often rented for extended stays or used by wedding parties, Joan Jones said. ❖ Continental breakfast is set out in the sunny breakfast room, where the ceiling is exposed brick. We helped ourselves to coffee, juice, melon, granola, cereal, English muffins, bagels, and coffee cake, and sat at small round bistro tables. Everything tasted fresh. Items were meticulously labeled, down to the brand of jam in ceramic pots. Arthur Jones chatted with us about the weather and our planned boat trip to the Isles of Shoals. ❖ The inn's other common room, dubbed "the gathering place," features a couch and chairs, lamps, and a CD player with a few CDs. It could be a place to escape if your partner wanted to take a nap or go to bed early. But you'd probably rather enjoy the bustling, historic city just outside your door.

ELLEN ALBANESE, *Globe Correspondent*

The Masthead

Getaway 44

31-41 Commercial St.,
Provincetown, Mass.
508-487-0523 or 800-395-5095
www.themasthead.com

RATES
21 rooms. Varies seasonally, $95-$352.

WHAT WE LIKED MOST
The ocean sunset just outside our front door.

WHAT WE LIKED LEAST
The ocean view dead ahead from our porch was blocked by a just-too-high white deck wall.

WHAT SURPRISED US
Our cottage's living room was larger than we expected.

YOU KNOW YOU'RE AT THE MASTHEAD WHEN... *fall's at full throttle, yet the nearness and sounds of the sea make you think it's summer.*

THINGS TO REMEMBER

IT WAS ODDLY REASSURING to find a copy of "Discrimination by Design: A Feminist Critique of the Man-Made Environment" at The Masthead resort. ❖ We like tradition, and the book by Leslie Kanes Weisman (University of Illinois, 1994) offered a sign that the town's historic solicitousness for the marginalized remains intact. ❖ But it was Provincetown's recently advertised pitch for family tourism that had brought us and our toddler to Cape Cod's fingertip. We were looking forward to enjoying an old town in a new way. ❖ The past is present in many ways at The Masthead. It has long catered to an elite clientele; our two-bedroom cottage — one of 21 cottages, apartments, and motel rooms — is named for Helena Rubinstein, who frequented here. At $252 a night, a cosmetic magnate's fortune would still come in handy, and even at that price, we got use of only the first floor, which became clear when we heard someone padding around above our ceiling. But the same digs would have run us $388 before Labor Day; more economical rooms are available. ❖ Besides, that price bought us a perch literally atop the ocean, which at high tide rushed under the pier on which our porch rested. Our door opened to an expansive view of Provincetown Harbor, stretched like a gargantuan smile between the dimples of the periphery beaches. The waves slapping the beach and the salt air almost fooled us into believing we'd come for summer's overture rather than its curtain call. ❖ Our cottage's agreeably large living room came with a TV screen almost as wide as the oriental rug on the floor. The TV blocked the fireplace, which was just as well, since fire regulations don't allow for its use. Radiators heat the cottage during the winter. ❖ The Masthead is a few blocks from several eating places and a 10-minute walk from Provincetown's restaurant-filled center. That proximity is a convenience for any tourist and almost a necessity for visitors toting small children. ❖ Three historic buildings that help define The Masthead experience stand out at night, when the lights of three Cape lighthouses can be seen across the harbor. One of them, a 200-year-old structure in Truro, is the first light seen by ocean liners making the Atlantic crossing as they approach the East Coast, or so we were told by The Masthead's owners. For us, the three lights enhanced the maritime feel as we sat on the porch after dark.

KATHLEEN BURGE, *Globe Staff*
RICH BARLOW, *Globe Correspondent*

Enchanted Nights B&B

Getaway 45

29 Wentworth St.,
Kittery, Maine
207-439-1489
www.enchantednights.org

RATES
Nine rooms. $60-$350.

WHAT WE LIKED MOST
Visiting with innkeepers' cats and guests' dogs.

WHAT WE LIKED LEAST
Limited public areas for lounging and chatting with other guests.

WHAT SURPRISED US
Awkward bathing facilities and no change of towels on second day, even though they'd been used to mop up the floor.

YOU KNOW YOU'RE AT ENCHANTED NIGHTS B&B WHEN ... *you have a satisfying vegetarian breakfast.*

THINGS TO REMEMBER
_____
_____
_____
_____

***MAINE · **NEW HAMPSHIRE · VERMONT · MASS**

AS WE PLANNED AN EARLY HOLIDAY shopping getaway to Kittery, the website of Enchanted Nights B&B seemed to promise the right combination of comfort, whimsy, and convenience. ❖ The property sits on quiet Kittery Point, just two miles from Kittery's strip of outlet malls, and the web copy described "colorful Country-French and Victorian decor" in an 1890 Princess Anne Victorian home. ❖ An overgrown yard and approaching darkness couldn't hide the multiple gables and very unMaine-like cream, pink, pale blue, and green palette. "We're still working on the color scheme," innkeeper Peter Lamandia told us when he unlocked the door and led us inside. ❖ While the inn has some bargain-priced rooms, we had splurged on "Sweet Dreams," one of two rooms with whirlpool tubs. It was tucked under the eaves on the third floor, up a steep, narrow, and dimly lighted staircase. ❖ We were greeted by cheerful yellow walls, a peaked ceiling accented with wooden beams, and three big windows. A comfortable queen bed with ornate wooden headboard sat on a rose-patterned carpet at one end. The bed was flanked by a matching armoire with mirrored doors, and a large marble-topped dresser with beveled mirror. A dressing table with full-length mirror stood near the foot of the bed. ❖ At the opposite end of the room, a large red whirlpool tub sat under sloping eaves painted with a charming mural of sky and clouds. A huge mirror covered the wall beside the whirlpool, a small sink hung on another wall, and a toilet was shoe-horned into a tight enclosure with a folding mirrored door. ❖ We had hoped for an early start in the morning, but the innkeepers declined to serve breakfast before 9. When we arrived in the dining area a few minutes before the hour, the other guests were already on their second cups of coffee. The tight quarters — there was even more furniture here than in our room — encouraged lively conversation. A couple from Michigan with their daughter from Manhattan were using the inn to spend a few days exploring the area. Lamandia brought out a tray with small bowls of blackberry cobbler, then arranged a buffet of toast and eggs scrambled with vegetables and vegetarian "ham." The Michigan couple were antiques hunters and were taken with the glassware, crocheted potholders, lamps and ceiling fixtures, and old furniture in the room. When we left for the outlet malls, Lamandia was filling them in on his favorite shops and lamenting pieces he hadn't bought. We were surprised that any had escaped.

PATRICIA HARRIS AND DAVID LYON, *Globe Correspondents*

Eagle Mountain House

Getaway 46

Carter Notch Road,
Jackson, N.H.
603-383-9111 or 800-966-5779
www.eaglemt.com

RATES
65 rooms and 30 suites.
Varies seasonally, $69-$229.

WHAT WE LIKED MOST
Sitting in the October sunshine on the veranda after eating waffles topped with maple butter.

WHAT WE LIKED LEAST
Inconsistent quality of the menu.

WHAT SURPRISED US
The antique elevator and its leisurely pace.

YOU KNOW YOU'RE AT EAGLE MOUNTAIN HOUSE WHEN... *you can see Carter Notch from the window of your room.*

THINGS TO REMEMBER
_____
_____
_____
_____

MAINE • NEW HAMPSHIRE • VERMONT • MASS

THE EAGLE MOUNTAIN HOUSE is one of New England's long-lived grand Victorian hotels. Like its cousins, the Mount Washington Resort at Bretton Woods and The Balsams Grand Resort Hotel, it is a sturdy, dignified place, with dark wood paneling, leather couches, portraits of earnest men, and a mighty veranda. But for all the grandeur and history, the Eagle Mountain House promotes itself as homey. My friend Kristen was quick to agree. "It reminds me of Grandma's house," she said as we sat down to breakfast on a Saturday in early autumn. ❖ I wasn't so sure. In the formal dining room, with its velvet drapes, forest-green walls, and antique chandeliers, I wondered whether I should be dabbing the corners of my mouth with a napkin and concentrating on keeping my elbows off the table. I imagined the generations of well-to-do Bostonians who had traveled to this perch in the White Mountains come summertime, their society manners and Brahmin ways transported from the sweltering city they could afford to escape. ❖ They would have been dabbing, I was certain. ❖ Antiques seem organic in this setting. It felt perfectly natural to ride a Portland Elevator Co. lift dating to circa 1916, its green metal door and black bars rattling and clanking as whining hydraulics lifted the contraption up and down, slowly but surely. Had a call come through the Western Electric telephone switchboard stretching across a wall behind the front desk, it would not have surprised. ❖ "She is a grand dame who has no pretensions about her age," said Jerry Jacobson, the inn's general manager. ❖ The hotel's history dates to 1879 when the Gale family, big landowners in the region, opened a guest house on their working farm. A fire in 1915 destroyed the building, and the Gales constructed a larger one on the site the next year. The building, five stories with white-clapboard siding and a 280-foot veranda, was smaller than other grand hotels, earning the title of "Baby Grand." ❖ Come morning, we were reluctant to leave, and we settled in by the lobby fireplace. ❖ Next to us sat Thomas Dudley, 76, a spry retired New Hampshire lawyer. He was a Dartmouth man, he told us, who had rejected Harvard. His mother had worked at the hotel, he said, and he had visited for his 25th wedding anniversary. He was back to mark the 50th. "It's a holdover from long ago," he said. "And that's reassuring."

SARAH SCHWEITZER, *Globe Staff*

Race Brook Lodge

Getaway 47

864 South Undermountain Road (Route 41), Sheffield, Mass.
413-229-2916 or 888-725-6343
www.rblodge.com

RATES
32 rooms and suites.
Varies seasonally, $80-$295.

WHAT WE LIKED MOST
The easy access to fantastic hiking.

WHAT WE LIKED LEAST
The street noise that filters into front-facing rooms.

WHAT SURPRISED US
The beautiful post-and-beam architecture that makes each room unique.

YOU KNOW YOU'RE AT RACE BROOK LODGE WHEN... *you notice the absence of traditional bed-and-breakfast frippery and frills.*

THINGS TO REMEMBER

MAINE • NEW HAMPSHIRE • VERMONT • MASS

ITS NICKNAME SAYS IT ALL: Hikers' Heaven. ❖ Just minutes by foot out the back door of the Race Brook Lodge, there is a dirt path that leads over a bridge, along a stream, up a hill, through a forest — and eventually to the Appalachian Trail and Mount Race, with its knockout views of the Housatonic River Valley and the Hudson River. ❖ And not once from bed to breakfast table to mountaintop will you have needed a car. ❖ The Berkshires have always felt a bit too precious for my taste — the Talbots store in downtown Lenox, the Mercedeses with New York plates gliding along the country lanes of Lee, the fussy mansion-inns dolled up with velvet and lace. It's all so excruciatingly proper. ❖ That's why I adore the quirky, outdoorsy Race Brook Lodge, which calls itself a "chintz-free rustic mountain hideaway," a description that couldn't be more apt. ❖ "Bed-and-breakfasts are famous for bath curtains and bedspreads and sheets that all match, and we're opposed to that," says David Rothstein, the lodge's wry, shaggy-haired owner. The lodge is as far from an antique-filled Victorian as can be. The main guesthouse is a restored post-and-beam barn with 15 rooms tucked into its nooks, carved out of its crannies, and wedged under its eaves. Each is different, and each is charming in its own way. Some are snug and cozy, others are airy and spacious. Most have plank floors and ceiling beams. None have phones or TVs. They're minimally decorated, with stenciling and little more. ❖ The downstairs of the main lodge is a sprawling common area where guests gather for a self-service buffet breakfast of mostly organic, all-natural foods. It's simple, delicious, healthy food that perfectly matches the earthy ambience. ❖ The oldest part of the lodge, which originally was a farm, dates to about 1790. Rothstein turned the place into an inn when he bought it in 1990, and he also owns the restaurant next door, the Stagecoach Tavern (stagecoachtavern.net). Don't be fooled by the "tavern" name; the aura is moodily elegant, the food is fancy, and the prices aren't cheap. ❖ The lodge, which also has an inground pool, makes a good base camp for exploring the museums, historic homes, farms, gardens, and galleries of the southern Berkshires. ❖ As for that nickname, it really is a heaven for hikers. In addition to the Mount Race trail, the lodge offers easy access to Bash Bish Falls State Park, Mount Everett, Mount Washington State Forest, Jug End State Reservation, and Monument Mountain.

SACHA PFEIFFER, *Globe Staff*

The Old Mystic Inn

Getaway 48

52 Main St.,
Old Mystic, Conn.
860-572-9422
www.oldmysticinn.com

RATES
Eight rooms. Varies seasonally, $125-$205. No children under age 15.

WHAT WE LIKED MOST
The well-stocked guest kitchen where we could help ourselves to beverages and microwave popcorn.

WHAT WE LIKED LEAST
The absence of a closet or an armoire; our 21st-century clothes on hangers took away from the room's 19th-century ambience.

WHAT SURPRISED US
Gourmet breakfasts, elegantly presented.

YOU KNOW YOU'RE AT THE OLD MYSTIC INN WHEN... you feel compelled to put down your paperback bestseller and delve into an antique tome.

THINGS TO REMEMBER

I WAS SITTING IN THE COZY keeping room of The Old Mystic Inn when innkeeper Michael S. Cardillo Jr. walked in, bent under a large wooden spinning wheel. ❖ Where would he put it, I wondered. ❖ The room was already thoughtfully furnished and decorated. There was a comfortable couch and wingback chair. Antique dolls and toys flanked a chiming clock on the mantel over the huge stone fireplace. A rustic basket held kindling. Despite the busyness of the decor, the elements somehow worked together to create a soothing effect. ❖ But, as he would tell me later, Cardillo never tires of collecting furniture and accessories that will enhance the 1784 house he maintains with such care. ❖ Once a bookstore, the inn has kept the literary theme in eight rooms named for early American writers. Four are in the main house and four in a carriage house added in 1988. With their high ceilings and country cottage decor, carriage house rooms feel a bit more modern, and two have whirlpool tubs. ❖ In the main house there is one guest room on the first floor, but the rest of the space is given over to the keeping room, a sunny dining room, and a remarkably well-stocked kitchen. ❖ We stayed in the Nathaniel Hawthorne Room, which has cream-colored walls, dusty rose trim, and stenciled border. The queen four-poster bed was topped with a floral comforter in mauve and green, with a plaid bed skirt in the same hues, accent pillows, and a teddy bear. (Teddy bears of varying sizes and ages appear throughout the inn.) Hawthorne was everywhere: On a decorated shelf, a teddy bear wearing a plaid cap and rimless spectacles perched next to a copy of "The Scarlet Letter." On the dresser were hardbound editions, with yellowed pages, of "Twice-Told Tales" and "The House of the Seven Gables." Even the room key was attached to a miniature pewter book inscribed with a Hawthorne quote from "The Marble Faun": "Time flies over us but leaves its shadow behind." ❖ Cardillo's attention to detail extends to the elegant gourmet breakfasts served between 8:30 and 9:30. On Saturday we enjoyed scrambled eggs with herbs, ham, and asparagus tips on English muffins, topped with a light goat cheese sauce and accompanied by crisp, savory roasted red bliss potatoes. On select off-season weekends, Cardillo, a graduate of the Culinary Institute of America, offers a dinner package. ❖ As we were leaving, we took one last look into the keeping room. The spinning wheel by the fireplace looked as though it had always been there.

ELLEN ALBANESE, *Globe Staff*

Shelter Harbor Inn

Getaway 49

10 Wagner Road,
Westerly, R.I.
401-322-8883 or 800-468-8883
www.shelterharborinn.com

RATES
24 rooms. Varies seasonally, $96-$238.

WHAT WE LIKED MOST
The excellent food and service in the inn's dining rooms.

WHAT WE LIKED LEAST
Housekeeping knocking on the door at 9:30 Saturday morning.

WHAT SURPRISED US
A wood-burning fireplace in the room.

YOU KNOW YOU'RE AT THE SHELTER HARBOR INN WHEN... *you can top off a day at your private beach with a soak in the rooftop hot tub or a game of regulation croquet.*

THINGS TO REMEMBER

MAINE · NEW HAMPSHIRE · VERMONT · MASS

DON'T LET THE PLAIN EXTERIOR of the Shelter Harbor Inn deceive you. Inside the rambling white building with pale blue shutters, you find quiet charm, excellent food, and fine service. ❖ Shelter Harbor is as much a restaurant as an inn, boasting that it serves breakfast, lunch, and dinner 365 days a year. Staff members make guests feel like family, perhaps because in so many cases families have returned to this comfortable, unpretentious inn year after year. "After 30 years," said innkeeper James Dey, "we're starting to see the children of our early guests coming back with their own families." ❖ Guest rooms are split between the main house, a farmhouse dating from 1810, and a renovated barn. Our second-floor room in the main house was modest in size, but a private deck doubled the space. There was a wood-burning fireplace at one end, the brick chimney rising to the ceiling. Though there was a cradle of wood on the hearth, we saw no kindling or matches and learned later that we needed to ask a member of the staff to light the fire. We were pleased by the strong water pressure in the shower, often lacking in older buildings. ❖ A guest information booklet gave the history of the inn — it was established in 1911 as the core of a community for musicians called "Music Colony," and the surrounding streets bear such names as Wagner, Handel, and Bach. ❖ From the rooftop hot tub, there's a distant view of the ocean and Block Island. There are locker rooms with showers and a grill on the rooftop deck. Guests can play on a regulation American six-wicket croquet court, putting green, boccie court, and two tennis courts. The inn provides weekday parking passes to its private beach in Weekapaug and a shuttle bus on weekends. ❖ In the sunny breakfast room overlooking the gardens, we enjoyed cranberry-orange scones, corned beef hash with poached eggs, and banana walnut French toast one morning, eggs Benedict and a red pepper, tomato, and fresh mozzarella omelet the next. On Saturday evening the dining room was full, testifying to the draw of the restaurant. The house salad was a slightly sweet blend of mesclun greens, sliced apples, julienne carrots, Gorgonzola, and toasted walnuts with a dried cranberry vinaigrette. We enjoyed pumpkin seed-crusted salmon with garlic lentils and spinach and a flat iron steak with roasted mushroom sauce. ❖ Then we took the rest of our wine upstairs and sat under the stars on our private deck, savoring the marriage of fine food and comfortable lodging.

ELLEN ALBANESE, *Globe* Staff

The Quechee Inn
at Marshland Farm

Getaway 50

1119 Quechee Main St.,
Quechee, Vt.
802-295-3133 or 800-235-3133
www.quecheeinn.com

RATES
22 rooms and three suites. $90-$245.

WHAT WE LIKED MOST
The idyllic country setting next to the Ottauquechee River.

WHAT WE LIKED LEAST
Molasses-slow service in the dining room at dinner.

WHAT SURPRISED US
His and her bathrooms in our room.

YOU KNOW YOU'RE AT THE QUECHEE INN WHEN . . . *you can shop for small antiques from cases in the lobby.*

THINGS TO REMEMBER
_____
_____
_____
_____
_____

MAINE · NEW HAMPSHIRE · VERMONT · MASS

IS THERE AN OLD BUILDING in New England that hasn't been placed on the National Register of Historic Places? Sure enough, when we reached the front door of the Quechee Inn, one of the ubiquitous bronze plaques proudly proclaimed that it had joined that august company. ❖ To be fair, the old farm, surrounded by majestic trees and white rail fences, borders on the iconic. The original portion of the boxy white clapboard inn was built in 1793 by Colonel Joseph Marsh, the first lieutenant governor of Vermont. He chose a prime spot along the Ottauquechee River to erect what neighbors called his "baronial mansion." ❖ Whatever airs Marsh might have affected, he ran a working farm, growing wheat and corn and cutting timber. The land continued to provide for its owners and successive herds of Jersey cattle well into the 20th century. Our room, No. 11, was on the second floor of the original home. Wide pine-plank floorboards grown amber with age set the tone. The walls were painted a subtle beige, and the king-size bed was laid with a beige and rose floral coverlet. Each of the two wing chairs in front of a pair of windows was flanked by a good reading light. ❖ A long second-story porch overlooks the property, but by early November we were more interested in the downstairs lounge, where hot drinks and cookies are set out every afternoon and taciturn portraits of early Marshes adorn the mantel above a brick fireplace. Even without the glow of the fire, the barnboard walls, brick floors, and beamed ceiling give the room a rustic warmth. ❖ The inn's country ambience continues in the dining room where a generous breakfast buffet (eggs, bacon, pancakes, home fries, muffins, fruit, etc.) is laid out each morning and the ivy-pattern wallpaper gives a cheerful touch to the large, low-ceilinged room. In the evening, dim incandescent lighting and white pillar candles flickering in hurricane globes create a soft mood. ❖ The dinner menu follows the culinary-school pattern of dressing up simple meats with exotic accoutrements. All attempts to be worldly disappeared at dessert: apple pie a la mode and cream puffs with ice cream and chocolate sauce. ❖ But that was for the best. The Quechee Inn is a true slice of Vermont, an honest farm more than a baronial manse. On our way upstairs, we saluted the Marshes, congratulating their clan for carving out a country home that ought to last another 200 years.

PATRICIA HARRIS AND DAVID LYON, *Globe Correspondents*

The Inn at Clamber Hill

Getaway 51

111 North Main St.,
Petersham, Mass.
978-724-8800 or 888-374-0007
www.clamberhill.com

RATES
Five rooms. Varies seasonally, $150-$310.

WHAT WE LIKED MOST
The elegance of our suite.

WHAT WE LIKED LEAST
A quibble, to be sure, but the pasta dinner could have used a sauce.

WHAT SURPRISED US
The spaciousness of our sitting room, affording our toddler room to roam.

YOU KNOW YOU'RE AT THE INN AT CLAMBER HILL WHEN... Sam and Shamrock, the owners' dogs, lead you on a walk into the back field.

THINGS TO REMEMBER

AS A TOURIST STOP, Central Massachusetts is something of a soft-focus blur. Unless you're catching an event at the DCU Center in Worcester, the Commonwealth's geographic bull's-eye doesn't beckon a visitor like historic Boston and Cape Cod to the east or the woods and waterways of the Berkshires to the west. ❖ But the hill country surrounding the Quabbin Reservoir boasts diversions to please everyone, from the outdoorsman to seekers of creature comforts. Falling squarely in the second camp, we spent two autumn nights at the Inn at Clamber Hill. ❖ Owners Mark and Deni Ellis alternately refer to their establishment as an inn or a bed-and-breakfast. Though the place technically qualifies as a B&B, with just five guest rooms, those who prefer the more spacious and elegant accommodations of an inn need not scratch Clamber Hill from their to-visit list. ❖ Built in the Roaring Twenties as a summer mansion by a Springfield couple, the Inn at Clamber Hill is the oversized kid in the B&B class. Its 9,600 square feet sprawl in a squared-off "U" flanked by two arched roofs as crisp as a Marine's trouser crease, reflecting Mark Ellis's former life as a member of the corps. ❖ Our four-footed welcoming committee included Sam and Shamrock, a golden retriever and a chow, respectively, as friendly as they were furry. There was also a house cat for feline admirers, and, to the delight of our toddler, two horses who could be admired up close and from a distance when they're set loose in the field down from the inn. There are 33 forested acres surrounding the estate that are laced with trails, and depending on the season, the property is a hiker's or cross-country skier's dream. ❖ The inn's literature said our suite, the European, was especially popular with honeymooners, and it's easy to see why a couple craving privacy wouldn't want to leave. Along with glass French doors and a decanter of brandy, there was a working fireplace fronted by a sofa, several original oil paintings, an antique desk, and a bedroom easy chair with ottoman for reading. ❖ We dined at the inn's tiny restaurant, where Mark Ellis does double duty as chef, on one of our two nights. Accommodating the family vegetarian, he prepared a pasta with vegetables. The sauceless dish could have used something to flavor it, but the inclusion of artichokes was an inspired complement to the noodles. Our carnivore rated as excellent the Chicken Clamber Hill, a take-off on chicken Cordon Bleu that could have easily turned greasy in less competent hands.

RICH BARLOW, *Globe Correspondent*

The Captain Lord Mansion

Getaway 52

6 Pleasant St.,
Kennebunkport, Maine
207-967-3141
www.captainlord.com

RATES
16 rooms. Varies seasonally, $166-$429.

WHAT WE LIKED MOST
The bathroom in the Champion Room is like a personal all-day spa.

WHAT WE LIKED LEAST
Breakfast is grand, but it's also communal and there is only a single breakfast time.

WHAT SURPRISED US
The basement gift shop had little treasures and curiosities tucked in every corner.

YOU KNOW YOU'RE AT THE CAPTAIN LORD MANSION WHEN... the only television is in a basement viewing lounge.

THINGS TO REMEMBER
_____
_____
_____
_____

MAINE · NEW HAMPSHIRE · VERMONT · MASS

THERE'S A LITTLE GIZMO on the wall that catches the eye as you walk into the bathroom of the Champion Room at The Captain Lord Mansion. ❖ Turns out, it's a knob that adjusts the temperature of the bathroom's floor tiles. ❖ Yes, when you stay in the Champion Room, or other accommodations at this inn, built in 1812 as a private residence, you decide just how toasty you want the bathroom floor. ❖ It's also indicative of the unique problem faced by anyone who stays at this richly appointed bed-and-breakfast. The inn is a short, pleasant walk from downtown Kennebunkport, which is crammed with shops, restaurants, cafes, and galleries, many of them open year-round. ❖ Therein lies the problem. Because the rooms and amenities at Captain Lord are so inviting, the visitor is tempted to never leave the property. Each of the 16 rooms in the main building is unique. Basics include wireless Internet and gas fireplaces, a mini-fridge stocked with complimentary waters, juices, and soft drinks, along with a CD player and a selection of new age/romantic-themed discs. ❖ Our room was chockablock with antiques, paintings, and other "stuff." The end result was far more "fun clutter" than claustrophobic. The luxurious king bed had a headboard with a painted farm scene. Our mini-fridge was on the floor of our cedar closet. ❖ The room was something special, but it paled in comparison to the bathroom. For starters, you could have ridden a horse into it. Along with the lighted walk-in marble shower, double pedestal vanities, and spa tub for two (accented with Roman columns), there was a fountain. ❖ Yes, a wall fountain, about 3-by-5 feet with water dribbling down a faux Roman fresco that conjured up past visits to Pompeii. ❖ Those who leave the room to amble around the inn will discover a great room with a large fireplace. Find the circular stairway near the front of the inn and you can ascend several floors to the enclosed widow's walk and a commanding view. The basement includes a television lounge, a newly built spa, and gift shop. There is no room service, but a communal three-course gourmet breakfast is served each day. ❖ There are plenty of reasons to leave The Captain Lord Mansion and take in all the sights and experiences unique to southern Maine. But the inn doesn't make heading out the door very easy.

DEAN JOHNSON, *Globe Correspondent*

CONNECTICUT

Grand Pequot Tower..22
Homestead Inn...16
The Old Mystic Inn...98
Tolland Inn..12
Watson House..32

MAINE

Bass Cottage Inn 78
The Captain Lord Mansion...106
Enchanted Nights B&B...92
Grey Havens Inn..66
The Inn on Peaks Island...52
Newcastle Inn..68
Norumbega Inn..10
Pentagoet Inn..62

MASSACHUSETTS

Beach Rose Inn..72
Captain Jack's Wharf..60
Chatham Wayside Inn..30
Cliff Lodge..98
Encore Bed & Breakfast...86
The Golden Slipper...50
Hotel Commonwealth..36
The Inn at Clamber Hill..104
The Lighthouse Inn...56
The Masthead..90
Ocean View Inn & Resort..58
Old Inn on the Green..14
Point Independence Inn..46
Race Brook Lodge...96
Red Maple Inn...80
Seacrest Manor...54
Sturbridge Country Inn..28
Warfield House Inn at Valley View Farm..................................74

NEW HAMPSHIRE

Ash Street Inn..24
Bow Street Inn...88
Eagle Mountain House...94
Inn at Crystal Lake...84
Inn at Danbury...82
The Inn at Thorn Hill and Spa..18
Riverbend Inn Bed & Breakfast..38
Victoria Inn..42

RHODE ISLAND

Blueberry Cove Inn..26
The Chanler at Cliff Walk...4
General Stanton Inn...40
Governor Bradford House Country Inn..48
Mowry-Nicholson House..34
The Richards..64
Shelter Harbor Inn..100

VERMONT

The Inn at Ormsby Hill..44
The Inn at Sawmill Farm..6
The Lauren...76
The Quechee Inn at Marshland Farm...102
Three Stallion Inn..8
Village Inn of Woodstock...20

52 WEEKS Dining Out
The Boston Globe
REVIEWS OF BOSTON

52 WEEKS Cheap Eats
The Boston Globe
REAL MEAL

52 WEEKS Checking In
The Boston Globe
Great Getaways!
FAVORITE PLACES TO STAY IN NEW ENGLAND 2008

Only $9.95 each!

Visit **BostonGlobeStore.com**

Eat.
Drink.
Stay awhile.

The Boston Globe Guidebooks Collection

Cheap Eats Recent reviews from The Globe's popular "Cheap Eats" column point you to a year's worth of delicious deals.

Dining Out Discover the best restaurants in the Boston area—from steakhouses to gourmet bistros and more.

Checking In Trust The Globe's award-winning *Travel* writers to help you find the perfect place to stay in New England.

Order now for just $9.95 each!

BUY MORE, SAVE MORE
Buy any 2 for $15.95;
complete set of 3 only $20.95!

or call **1.888.665.2667**.

The Boston Globe STORE